Primary Source Readings in

Catholic Social Justice

Primary Source Readings in
Catholic Social Justice

Jerry Windley-Daoust

saint mary's press

This book is dedicated to the Winona Catholic Worker for help with this book, for its commitment for doing justice in the Catholic Tradition, and for the inspiration the organization is to us all.

The publishing team included Steven C. McGlaun, development editor; Lorraine Kilmartin, reviewer; Mary Koehler, permissions editor; prepress and manufacturing coordinated by the prepublication and production services departments of Saint Mary's Press.

Design Pics Images / Fotosearch, cover image

Printed in the United States of America

1347

ISBN 978-0-88489-968-6

Library of Congress Cataloging-in-Publication Data

Windley-Daoust, Jerry.
    Primary source readings in Catholic social justice / Jerry Windley-Daoust.
    p. cm.
ISBN: 978-0-88489-968-6 (pbk.)
    1. Social justice—Religious aspects—Catholic Church. 2. Catholic Church—
Doctrines. I. Title.
BX1795.J87W57 2007
261.8088'282—dc22

                                                      2006030481

Contents

Introduction

This book isn't finished. Yes, I know it doesn't *look* unfinished—it's full of words, cover to cover. And not just any words, either, but words that are meant to change the world. You may have noticed that a lot of those words come from popes and bishops—they're part of the Catholic social teaching tradition.

What? You haven't heard of Catholic social teaching? Well, don't worry. . . . It *has* been called the Church's best-kept secret. Okay, crash course: Basically, Catholic social teaching got its start in the late nineteenth century as a response to the social problems created by the Industrial Revolution. You might recall from history class that mechanized production put a lot of people out of work, while those who found work in factories put in twelve- to sixteen-hour days for extremely low pay. Not surprisingly, the workers weren't too thrilled with this arrangement.

Before long, Karl Marx and Friedrich Engels were suggesting that the workers could solve their problems by taking over the factories, throwing the owners out on their collective ears, and getting rid of religion while they were at it. Quite a few people found those ideas pretty appealing, but a handful of Catholics thought they could do better. Calling themselves the Fribourg Union (because they met in Fribourg, Switzerland, every year), they tried applying the Gospel and the Catholic theological tradition to modern social problems. Pope Leo XIII liked their ideas, incorporated them into his 1891 encyclical *On Capital and Labor (Rerum Novarum)*, and voila, everyone lived happily ever after.

Well, okay, not really. But *On Capital and Labor* did make a difference, especially the bit about the dignity of workers and their right to organize unions. In fact, *On Capital and Labor* was such a hit that as new problems cropped up, the Church kept writing about them in light of the Scriptures and Catholic Tradition. That's what we call Catholic social teaching (or social doctrine), which the Church recently summarized in a neat little book called the *Compendium of the Social Doctrine of the Church*. The themes of each chapter in this book correspond to the themes of the twelve chapters in the *Compendium*, which is handy if you want to use them together.

Besides Catholic social teaching, this book is also full of words from people who took that teaching and ran with it. Folks like Marion Maendel, Kim Dae-jung, Sr. Helen Prejean, and Archbishop Oscar Romero are good examples of how the ideas in Catholic social teaching can change the way people relate to one another. Other folks, like Julie Hanlon Rubio and Cardinal Joseph Bernardin, extend the insights of Catholic social teaching into new territory. And a few, with their own ideas, have actually influenced the way Catholics do social justice.

Within these pages, you will also find ideas that might challenge the way you see the world around you. These moments when you are challenged are precisely the reason to be reading this book. The social teachings of the Church are not always comfortable, and they are most definitely not easy. By grappling with these truths, you will more fully understand the teachings of the Church and yourself.

But back to the business of this unfinished book. This book is indeed full of words, but they are not the sort of words that are meant to be read and then left for dead on the page like one might do with a mystery novel. These words will be fully spoken only when they take root in a compassionate heart, and come to life in loving actions. That's the way it is with the Gospel—alive, not dead on a page, always writing something new in the world. And it's someone a whole lot like you— yes, you (stop looking over your shoulder!)—who is called to write the next story of how God's love and justice take on flesh and blood in the here and now.

"Tell them how to use this book," my editor says. Okay, ready? (1) Read the words. (2) Figure out how those words might change you. (Answering the questions at the end of each chapter might help. Wouldn't hurt to pray a little, either.) (3) Go out there and bring the word to life in the world. (4) Stand back and stay alert—you might just witness a miracle or two.

Mother Teresa

God's Plan of Love for Humanity

Introduction

After graduating from high school, Marion Maendel set out to save the world. She started by becoming a live-in volunteer at Casa Juan Diego, a Catholic Worker House of Hospitality in Houston, Texas, that provides Christian hospitality to the local Hispanic community, especially migrants and refugees. She began her work full of idealism and self-confidence, but that quickly began to fade as her dreams ran up against the gritty reality of the people she served. A year into her work at Casa Juan Diego, a corporate executive she met on an airplane made a prediction: "In about five years, maybe sooner, you are going to burn out and quit. . . . You are going to run out of idealism first. You are going to become hard and cynical, and realize that people are cruel and thankless and undeserving s.o.b.s. And then you'll get a real job."

As Maendel relates in her essay, which is excerpted in this chapter, that is not exactly what happened. But the businessman has a point. At times, people definitely *can* be cruel and thankless and undeserving. So why should we do anything to help others, much less try to save the world? And if

Second Vatican Council:

The Second Vatican Council was an ecumenical council (that is, a council of the whole Church) convened by Pope John XXIII in 1962 to find new ways of understanding and expressing divine revelation. Guided by the Holy Spirit, the Council led to many changes in the Church, including its worship and relationship to the rest of the world.

we do try to make a difference, what will keep us from becoming hard, cynical, and burnt out?

Like Maendel, the Church is out to save the world. "The joys and hopes, the grief and anguish of the people of our time, especially of those who are poor or afflicted, are the joys and hopes, the grief and anguish of the followers of Christ as well," the Second Vatican Council declares at the beginning of its *Pastoral Constitution on the Church in the Modern World (Gaudium et Spes)*. "Nothing that is genuinely human fails to find an echo in their hearts" (no. 1). Motivated by this compassion, the Council went on to examine the various problems facing the modern world, and to offer principles for just and peaceful solutions.

If *The Church in the Modern World* had been a business plan, the corporate executive who warned Maendel might have called it impossibly idealistic and doomed to failure. But in carrying out its mission in the world, the Church does not follow a business plan. Nor is it driven by an idealistic belief in the power of humans to achieve true justice and peace on their own. Rather, the way it works for justice and peace is by cooperating with God's plan of love for humanity. As the Council says in *The Church in the Modern World*, that plan sheds light on the true identity and ultimate destiny of every human person. It also reveals that people can overcome the effects of sin—including the world's cruelty and our own cynicism—only with God's help.

As you read excerpts from *The Church in the Modern World*, consider what each paragraph says about (1) who human beings are and (2) what they are called to do, in light of God's plan. As Marion Maendel discovered, it is only in this light that we can begin to make things right, which is what justice is all about.

Excerpts from *Pastoral Constitution on the Church in the Modern World (Gaudium et Spes)*

by the Second Vatican Council

Preface

Humanity's Deeper Questionings

The dichotomy affecting the modem world is, in fact, a symptom of the deeper dichotomy that is rooted in humanity itself. It is the meeting point of many conflicting forces. As created beings, people are subject to many limitations, but they feel unlimited in their desires and their sense of being destined for a higher life. They feel the pull of many attractions and are compelled to choose between them and reject some among them. Worse still, feeble and sinful as they are, they often do the very thing they hate and do not do what they want. And so they feel themselves divided, and the result is a host of discords in social life. Many, it is true, fail to see the dramatic nature of this state of affairs in all its clarity for their vision is in fact blurred by materialism, or they are prevented from even thinking about it by the wretchedness of their plight. Others delude themselves that they have found peace in a world-view now fashionable. There are still others whose hopes are set on a genuine and total emancipation of humankind through human effort alone and look forward to some future earthly paradise where all the desires of their hearts will be fulfilled. Nor is it unusual to find people who, having lost faith in life, extol the kind of foolhardiness which would empty life of all significance in itself and invest it with a meaning of their own devising. Nonetheless, in the face of modern developments there is a growing body of people who are asking the most fundamental of all questions or are glimpsing them with a keener insight: What is humanity? What is the meaning of suffering, evil, death, which have not been eliminated by all this progress? What is the purpose of these achievements, purchased at so high a price? What can people contribute to society? What can they expect from it? What happens after this earthly life is ended?

The church believes that Christ, who died and was raised for the sake of all, can show people the way and strengthen them through the Spirit so that they become worthy of their destiny: nor is there given any other name under heaven by which they can be saved. The church likewise believes that the key, the center and the purpose of the whole of human history is to be found in its Lord and Master. It also maintains that beneath all those changes there is much that is unchanging, much that has its ultimate foundation in Christ, who is the same yesterday, and today, and forever. And that is why the council, relying on the inspiration of Christ, the image of the invisible God, the firstborn of all creation, proposes to speak to all people in order to unfold the mystery that is humankind and cooperate in tackling the main problems facing the world today. . . .

Part I

Chapter 1: The Dignity of the Human Person

Women and Men in the Image of God

Believers and unbelievers agree almost unanimously that all things on earth should be ordained to humanity as to their center and summit.

But what is humanity? People have put forward, and continue to put forward, many views about humanity, views that are divergent and even contradictory. Sometimes they either set it up as the absolute measure of all things, or debase it to the point of despair. Hence humanity's doubt and anguish. The church is keenly sensitive to these difficulties. Enlightened by divine revelation it can offer a solution to them by which the true state of humanity may be described, its weakness explained in such a way that at the same time its dignity and vocation may be perceived in their true light. For sacred scripture teaches that women and men were created "in the image of God," able to know and love their creator, and set by him over all earthly creatures that they might rule them, and make use of them, while glorifying God. "What are women and men that you are mindful of them, their sons and daughters that you care for them? You have made them little less than angels, and crown them with glory and honor. You have given them dominion over the works of your hands; you have put all things under their feet" (Ps 8:5–8).

But God did not create men and women as solitary beings. From the beginning "male and female God created them" (Gen 1:27). This partnership of man and woman constitutes the first form of communion between people. For by their innermost nature men and women are social beings; and if they do not enter into relationships with others they can neither live nor develop their gifts.

So God, as we read again in the Bible, saw "all the things that he had made, and they were very good" (Gen 1:31).

Sin

Although set by God in a state of righteousness, men and women, enticed by the evil one, abused their freedom at the very start of history. They raised themselves up against God, and tried to attain their goal apart from him. Although they had known God, they did not glorify him as God, but their senseless hearts were darkened, and they served the creature rather than the creator. What revelation makes known to us is confirmed by our own experience. For when people look into their own hearts they find that they are drawn towards what is wrong and are sunk in many evils which cannot have come from their good creator. Often refusing to acknowledge God as their source, men and women have also upset the relationship which should link them to their final destiny; and at the same time they have broken the right order that should exist within themselves as well as between them and other people and all creatures.

They are therefore divided interiorly. As a result, the entire life of women and men, both individual and social, shows itself to be a struggle, and a dramatic one, between good and evil, between light and darkness. People find that they are unable of themselves to overcome the assaults of evil successfully, so that everyone feels as if in chains. But the Lord himself came to free and strengthen humanity, renewing it inwardly and casting out the "prince of this world" (Jn 12:31), who held it in the bondage of sin. For sin diminished humanity, preventing it from attaining its fulfillment.

Both the high calling and the deep misery which people experience find their final explanation in the light of this revelation.

Humanity's Essential Nature

. . . Women and men are not mistaken when they regard themselves as superior to merely bodily creatures and as more than mere particles of nature or nameless units in human society. For by their power to know themselves in the depths of their being they rise above the entire universe of mere objects. When they are drawn to think about their real selves they turn to those deep recesses of their being where God who probes the heart awaits them, and where they themselves decide their own destiny in the sight of God. So when they recognize in themselves a spiritual and immortal soul, this is not an illusion, a product of their imagination, to be explained solely in terms of physical or social causes. On the contrary, they have grasped the profound truth of the matter. . . .

Kinds of Atheism and Its Causes

Human dignity rests above all on the fact that humanity is called to communion with God. The invitation to converse with God is addressed to men and women as soon as they are born. For if people exist it is because God has created them through love, and through love continues to keep them in existence. They cannot live fully in the truth unless they freely acknowledge that love and entrust themselves to their creator. . . .

Christ the New Man

In reality it is only in the mystery of the Word made flesh that the mystery of humanity truly becomes clear. For Adam, the first man, was a type of him who was to come, Christ the Lord. Christ the new Adam, in the very revelation of the mystery of the Father and of his love, fully reveals humanity to itself and brings to light its very high calling. It is no wonder, then, that all the truths mentioned so far should find in him their source and their most perfect embodiment.

He who is the "image of the invisible God" (Col 1:15), is himself the perfect man who has restored in the children of Adam that likeness to God which had been disfigured ever since the first sin. Human nature, by the very fact that it was assumed, not absorbed, in him, has been raised in us also to a dignity beyond compare. For, by his incarnation, he, the Son of God, has in a certain way united himself with each individual. He worked with human hands, he thought with a human mind. He acted with a human will and with a human heart he loved. Born of the Virgin Mary, he has truly been made one of us, like to us in all things except sin.

As an innocent lamb he merited life for us by his blood which he freely shed. In him God reconciled us to himself and to one another, freeing us from the bondage of the devil and of sin, so that each one of us could say with the apostle: the Son of God "loved me and gave himself for me" (Gal 2:20). By suffering for us he not only gave us an example so that we might follow in his footsteps, but he also opened up a way. If we follow this path, life and death are made holy and acquire a new meaning.

Conformed to the image of the Son who is the firstborn of many brothers and sisters, Christians receive the "first fruits of the Spirit" (Rom 8:23) by which they are able to fulfill the new law of love. By this Spirit, who is the "pledge of our inheritance" (Eph 1:14), the entire person is inwardly renewed, even to the "redemption of the body" (Rom 8:23). "If the Spirit of him who raised Jesus from the dead dwells in you, God who raised Christ Jesus from the dead will give life to your mortal bodies also through his Spirit who dwells in you" (Rom 8:11). The Christian is certainly bound both by need and by duty to struggle with evil through many afflictions and to suffer death; but, as one who has been made a partner in the paschal mystery, and as one who has been configured to the death of Christ, will go forward, strengthened by hope, to the resurrection.

All this holds true not only for Christians but also for all people of good will in whose hearts grace is active invisibly. For since Christ died for everyone, and since all are in fact called to one and the same destiny, which is divine, we must hold that the holy Spirit offers to all the possibility of being made partners, in a way known to God, in the paschal mystery.

Such is the nature and the greatness of the mystery of humankind as enlightened for the faithful by the Christian revelation. It is therefore through Christ, and in Christ, that fight is thrown on the mystery of suffering and death which, apart from his Gospel, overwhelms us. Christ has risen again, destroying death by his death, and has given life abundantly to us so that, becoming sons in the Son, we may cry out in the Spirit: Abba, Father! . . .

Chapter 2: The Human Community

Communitarian Nature of the Human Vocation: God's Design

God, who has a parent's care for all of us, desired that all men and women should form one family and deal with each other as brothers and sisters. All, in fact, are destined to the very same end, namely God himself, since they have been created in the likeness of God, who "made from one every nation of humankind who live on all the face of the earth" (Acts 17:26). Love of God and of one's neighbor, then, is the first and greatest commandment. Scripture teaches us that love of God cannot be separated from love of one's neighbor: "Any other commandment [is] summed up in this sentence: 'You shall love your neighbor as yourself . . .' therefore love is the fulfilling of the law" (Rom 13:9–10; see 1 Jn 4:20). It goes without saying that this is a matter of the utmost importance to people who are coming to rely more and more on each other and to a world which is becoming more unified every day.

Furthermore, the Lord Jesus, when praying to the Father "that they may all be one . . . even as we are one" (Jn 17:21–22), has opened up new horizons closed to human reason by indicating that there is a certain similarity between the union existing among the divine persons and the union of God's children in truth and love. It follows, then, that if human beings are the only creatures on earth that God has wanted for their own sake, they can fully discover their true selves only in sincere self-giving.

"Dorothy Day's Pilgrimage Continues at Casa Juan Diego: The Pilgrimage Continues . . . Poor Teach Harsh and Dreadful Love: A Disillusioned Catholic Worker Stays On"

by Marion Maendel

Marion Maendel came to Casa Juan Diego from the Bruderhof. She was baptized into the Catholic Church in March 2000.

It's another suffocating Houston night. Air, warm and thick as smoke, cloaks the city and settles in folds between the buildings on Rose Street. I sit in my second-story room in Casa Juan Diego House of Hospitality, fan stirring the heat, and read my journal of two years ago.

The entries cover my first months' experience here, and the writing is definitely familiar. The leaky green pen I remember as well, but the words printed across the college ruled notebook are those of a stranger. Who is this naïve do-gooder, so clinically diagnosing "problems in society" and outlining plans for "helping others?" And those dreams, the square solid expectations and fluffy quotes about serving the poor— I can't even imagine what they once meant. Smiling, I turn the page.

Outside in the night, a police siren shatters the heavy stillness. My ceiling twirls with red and blue flashing lights, and without looking, I can visualize the scene below my window. Two or three men, quite drunk, lie with cheeks pressed to the warm concrete, hands cuffed behind, as an officer barks commands in very bad Spanish. Leaning into the shadow of the laundromat wall, a handful of the male prostitutes are snickering quietly.

I return to the journal. It's littered with words as empty as the pages they're written on: "world suffering," "the poor," "social transformation." My eyes wander over a tidy commentary on "justice," then drift again with the heavy thump and twang of Tejano music coming from next door. That's Sonia's room. She's a sweet, dark-eyed sixteen-year-old from El Salvador, battered and pregnant by her twenty-three-year old "boyfriend." And homeless. And scared.

Again I try to concentrate. But now a gasp like a knife comes through the thin drywall, and sobbing, hard, choked, muffled in a pillow, follows after. It mocks the crisp words in front of me. I stand up and shut off the fan.

"Sonia, m'ija, what's up?"

The journal lands in the trash.

I have begun my third year here as a Catholic Worker. Arriving at Casa Juan Diego fresh out of high school, I had the classic "messiah complex," and

m'ija:

Spanish for "my daughter" or "my dear"

felt ready to save the world. Becoming a member of a vibrant volunteer movement equipped with enormous facilities, and widely known in the Hispanic community did little to convince me otherwise. As I immersed myself in Catholic Worker philosophy, study and discussions, I became enamored with the idea of "serving the poor" and "working for justice."

Then I met the people. They were poor, yes, and undeniably oppressed, downtrodden and desperate. I had counted on that. But I was unprepared for their concrete humanity, their sheer individuality as persons. They refused to be categorized as passive "problems" simply because I had appointed myself "helper." My well-heeled, condescending donation of time and surplus kindness was despicable in their eyes, and they were not desperate enough to bow and scrape around it for survival's sake.

It was the very people I came to "help" who began to teach me that acknowledgement of our common humanity under the pure gaze of God was the first and only point at which our mutual liberation could blossom. "We must be saved together," I read from Dorothy Day, and the smooth shell of my idealism began to splinter.

A year went by. On the plane trip back from summer vacation, I found myself sitting next to a businessman, who introduced himself as the CEO of a massive German graphic arts company.

"I'm a Catholic Worker volunteer," I nodded and quickly outlined the CW movement.

Reinart was fascinated. "Tell me about your work, the people," he begged. I told. He was silent and gazed out the window for a moment. "Let me tell you something," he said finally. "I admire your courage. I admire your idealism. But I will predict something, too. In about five years, maybe sooner, you are going to burn out and quit."

A little question mark of worry began to tingle in my stomach. It had been a long, luxurious vacation in the country. The thought of returning to inner city sordidness was suddenly terribly tiring, the endless dark parade of problems and demands, terrifying.

"Maybe," I conceded, "But how so?"

"Easy. You are going to run out of idealism first. You are going to become hard and cynical, and realize that people are cruel and thankless and undeserving s.o.b.s. And then you'll get a real job."

I stared at the seat in front of me. I thought of Marina, a battered woman with two children we had taken in a year ago. Besides giving her unlimited time with us to reorganize her life, we'd arranged work for her, counseling sessions, medical care, and legal assistance. One day she went to a close priest friend of ours, crying that we'd kicked her out without warning, and never done a thing to help. I remembered Vinny, who had run away from our youth house one night, taking with him every single one of our hard-won, portable electrical appliances. The seat in front of me blurred.

"Reinart," I said, "I think my idealism ran out my first month at work."

He nearly choked on his coffee. Reinart could respectfully dismiss my transient idealism, but the possibility of another sustaining force had his immediate attention.

"So what's left?" he demanded, and his eyes were suddenly fierce.

"Absolutely nothing." The words came hard, but I knew in that moment of resignation a relief as fine and pure as cold water. In acknowledging that my shaky fortress of idealism now lay in ruins, I finally allowed myself to be vulnerable. My "I know, you don't" approach to those whom I intended to save crumpled, and I became weaker, not more elite. I was shocked to discover that I, too, was desperately needy, empty, poor. And with the death of my belief in "the cause," came the assurance of another sort of stability, this no longer blind and shifting, but open, painfully open, and solid like a rock. Into that gaping wound rushed a healing liberation, a new forgiveness, a fresh capacity to love and be loved in faith, with God as the Source of compassion this time, not myself. It is a faith I still do not wholly possess, but it flits above the outstretched hand of my heart like a bright butterfly, and I know it to be the truth.

To have the vision in our hearts and minds of a new social order where love and justice truly reign is imperative, yes. This vision is usually what compels us to examine our lives so that we may live, work and love in a manner consistent with the Kingdom of God, and it can reveal to us the concrete, practical ways of conversion. But if such a vision remains in the abstract realm alone, it is useless, and eventually becomes an obstacle to any real transformation or liberation, whether personal or social.

It is easy to be in love with a concept; "mankind," "the poor," "the masses," for such abstractions hold all the seductiveness and untainted security of a fantasy. But when they encounter the concrete man, the concrete poor person, their cleanness is revealed as emptiness, their whiteness as sterility, and their sweetness as a cheap perfume which evaporates too quickly.

Tolstoy tells the story of a trainload of Communist agitators on their way to a Siberian labor camp. All of them have glorious dreams for the creation of a new society, where each will live in beatific harmony, justice and peace with his neighbor. But so removed are their ideals from the filth and chaos and humanity around them that they cannot translate into a single loving action. As the train rattles on through the icy night, they refuse to even make eye contact.

The inevitable disillusionment we experience early on in our journey here leaves us in a bleak, inner winter, but we can allow its empty ground to provide the spring seedbed for a truer love, the "harsh and dreadful love" talked of by Dostoyevsky and Dorothy Day. This love is active, with little use for visionary dreaming.

If I truly believe in the dignity of the human being, then I must also believe in the dignity of the bag lady waiting in our entrance hall, who complains that she doesn't like what I got her for dinner, and demands a tour of the accommodations before settling in. If I want to write about justice on my computer, I need to realize that the extra sweatshirts in my closet are property belonging to Sonia next door.

Purely philosophical dreams of love and justice are only given meaning when we begin to know poor people as people, and not obstacles, or objects to be acted upon. Then, slowly perhaps, can a society where love and justice flourish as by-products begin to grow. Cuban-American theologian Roberto Goizueta, has called this phenomenon the "scandal of particularity," where only the option for poor persons, not "the poor" exists.

The particular is indeed a scandal. "People come to join us in our 'wonderful work,'" Dorothy Day once said. "It all sounds very wonderful, but life itself is a haphazard, untidy, messy affair." Here we are confronted with inconveniences, frustrations and concrete rewards unknown to dreams. Helping a child walk for the first time, celebrating survival on New Year's Eve with a group of battered women, appreciating the relief of a starving, footsore immigrant family as they collapse on the sofas in the entrance after weeks of walking attests to a Gospel message rooted in the sacramentality of the human experience.

Faced with such raw distress, we must sometimes let go of all preconceived responses to a person's difficulties, including the desires to play savior or superman, and only let the pain rip into our hearts like a pruning hook. We must let it slash off the dead limbs of our coldness, cynicism and self-dependency to prepare for the new growth of compassion. Sometimes all we can do is weep in the brokenness of our human condition.

In this spirit, we learn with our guests to accompany the condemned Jesus of the poor, who wept for the world. Rather than let our lack of answers drive us to despair or anger, we can simply weep with and for Ricardo, whose teenage son was killed in gang crossfire; for Sara, fifteen, raped, pregnant, and kicked out of her house by incredulous parents; for Lupe, with her eyes swollen shut from spouse abuse; for Agustino, who rang the clinic doorbell yesterday, blood dripping from his clumsily slashed wrists—"I did it, I did it again"—his eyes huge with a child's terror.

Some nights I hold my head and ask myself, and God, what it is I think I'm doing here. We are, in the countless eyes of our critics, a foolishly blind group of idealists, obsessed with band-aid work. No amount of food, clothing, shelter, the "works of mercy" can stop the flow of desperate people that pours through our door. No amount of love, understanding, patience, giving, can immunize against the cruelty of human nature.

And yet, when I feel we can give no longer, when I want to turn my back on the whole business, when my utter inability to love frightens me so, and the futility of perseverance jeers, then, in that singular moment of brokenness, comes the still, small voice of the spat-upon Christ. And it chides me for thinking I can do this on my own, for hoping I can change people when I cannot even change myself. It shows up my small cold heart which I don't want to see, and then it offers me the redemptive Love of God forever young, which gives of itself, and gives, and gives, and gives and gives, without weighing the benefit, without considering the worthiness of the recipient, without imposing conditions and worldly calculations of immediate results. And in that "useless" Poverty of Inefficient Love, and only in it, I can go on.

Thus we work out our liberation with fear and trembling. And laughter. And hope. And we each cast our little pebble, as Dorothy said, into the pool of humanity, and watch the rings expand, knowing that in God's upside-down Kingdom, every menial task done in this Love is graced with an eternal significance.

Several days ago I was working in the dental clinic assisting with a routine filling on Julio, a street crack addict who worked nights as a prostitute. As I took his patient bib off, and told him we were done, he continued to sit in the chair.

"What is it?" I asked.

He shook off the daze and got up. Then he picked up his baseball cap, put it on firmly backwards, walked to the door—and turned back.

"I guess . . . pues, I've just never been treated this well before."

His grin was crooked, and he was near tears.

pues:

Spanish for "well"

For Reflection

1. Reinart, the businessman Maendel encountered on the plane, viewed people as "cruel and thankless and undeserving s.o.b.s." Respond to his statement by explaining the Church's view of the human person as it is expressed in *The Church in the Modern World*.
2. How did Maendel's attitude about "saving the world" change as a result of her work at Casa Juan Diego? How are her insights reflected in *The Church in the Modern World*? Provide specific examples by quoting from each reading.
3. What do you think is the most important truth in these readings? How is this truth important in your own life?

Profile

Mother Teresa: Ambassador of God's Love

On August 16, 1948, Mother Teresa left the convent school where she had been a teacher and principal for more than fifteen years. She loved teaching, but during a train ride to a retreat two years earlier, she had vividly experienced Jesus's distress at the abandonment of the poor— and his clear call for her to help them. When she began that mission, she had no companions, no possessions, and no detailed plan. She only knew that she was called to take seriously the words of Jesus: "Just as you did it to one of the least of these [poor] . . . you did it to me" (Matthew 25:40).

She began by starting a "school" that met under a tree in the slums of Calcutta, India. Eventually, some of her former students joined her, and others offered financial support. In 1950, the Vatican approved her new religious order, the Missionaries of Charity.

The new order soon became famous for serving the dying poor. If the sisters found a man lying in the gutter, dying, they would pick him up and carry him back to their Home for the Dying. There, they would bathe him and provide him with basic medical care. More important, they would treat him with dignity, respect, and love. Over the years, Mother Teresa founded homes for drug addicts, prostitutes, battered women, orphans, and those dying of AIDS.

As her fame spread, thousands of women and men joined the Missionaries of Charity as vowed religious sisters and brothers; more than a million others joined her as lay Co-Workers. She received more than 120 awards, including the Nobel Peace Prize. When she addressed the United Nations in 1985, the secretary general introduced her as the most powerful woman in the world.

Mother Teresa used her fame to speak out against abortion, war, and the death penalty. But she insisted that her primary mission was to love Jesus in the disguise of society's outcasts. In so doing, she and her companions vividly proclaimed to the world God's love for every person. Mother Teresa was beatified (that is, named blessed) by Pope John Paul II in 2003, just six years after her death.

Oscar Romero

The Church's Mission and Social Doctrine

Introduction

The power of the Church's social teaching lies in its ability to apply the Gospel—the Good News of Jesus Christ—to modern problems in a way that opens new, life-giving possibilities for the future. Such was the power that Archbishop Oscar Romero brought to the crisis facing El Salvador in the late 1970s. When he was assassinated by the government in 1980, it was not because he led a rebel army or encouraged violence, but because he shed the light of the Gospel on the suffering of the Salvadoran people.

In El Salvador, most people worked on plantations. Only a few actually owned the land, which had been forcibly taken from peasant farmers during the colonial period in order to grow cash crops for export. Though the landowners grew rich and powerful, almost everyone else lived in extreme poverty. This situation led to occasional peasant revolts, all of which were put down by the government.

Beginning in the 1970s, several Marxist groups began waging a guerrilla war against the military government. At the same time, many people in the Church began working directly with the peasants to relieve their suffering and win basic human rights. The landowners who ran the country saw both of these movements as a threat to their power, launching a campaign of brutal, random violence to suppress any call for change.

During the thirty-two years that he served as a parish priest, Romero supported the status quo in both the Church and society, and was suspicious of any attempt to change things. But he gradually began to change his views when he was appointed bishop of a rural diocese in

1974. In that role, he encountered poor workers on a regular basis. As he became more aware of their plight, he began using the resources of the diocese and his own personal resources to help meet their needs. He also began speaking out about the violence that was being perpetrated against those who spoke up for their rights.

When he was appointed archbishop of San Salvador in 1977, he was viewed by the ruling elite as a safe and conservative replacement for the previous archbishop. Less than a month later, though, a priest was gunned down for his role in organizing peasants. Murdered alongside the priest was another man and a seven-year-old boy. Stunned and outraged, Romero excommunicated the perpetrators from the Church and cancelled Sunday masses everywhere but the cathedral. Some 100,000 people attended the cathedral that Sunday to hear Romero condemn the oppression of the people.

The violence only grew worse; thousands of El Salvadorans were killed or tortured. Others simply disappeared, kidnapped by security forces in the night. Romero began regularly speaking out against this violence during hour-long weekly homilies that were broadcast by radio across the country. His words gave hope to ordinary people, who applauded him wherever he went.

Some of those in power became increasingly critical of Romero and others in the Church who defended the rights of the poor. He responded to these critics in his homilies and four pastoral letters. In his second pastoral letter, written just a few months after he became archbishop, he argues that the mission of the Church is to proclaim the Gospel and to be the Body of Christ in history. It would be impossible for the Church to carry out that mission—to be like Christ—without addressing the injustice, poverty, and violence of its time. That was essentially the same conclusion bishops from around the world reached in their 1971 synod. The document they issued, *Justice in the World*, says that "action on behalf of justice" is essential, not optional, in the preaching of the Gospel and the Church's mission in the world (no. 6).

On March 24, 1980, Romero was shot through the heart while saying Mass. The millions of people who mourned him took comfort in the Gospel he had read just moments before being killed: "Truly, truly, I say to you, unless a grain of wheat falls into the earth and dies, it remains alone; but if it dies, it bears much fruit" (John 12:24). Among the many fruits of Romero's life is a lasting reminder of what it really means to continue the mission of Christ in the world.

Excerpts from *Justice in the World*

by the World Synod of Catholic Bishops

Introduction

1. Gathered from the whole world, in communion with all who believe in Christ and with the entire human family, and opening our hearts to the Spirit who is the whole of creation new, we have questioned ourselves about the mission of the People of God to further justice in the world.

2. Scrutinizing the "signs of the times" and seeking to detect the meaning of emerging history, while at the same time sharing the aspirations and questionings of all those who want to build a more human world, we have listened to the Word of God that we might be converted to the fulfilling of the divine plan for the salvation of the world.

3. Even though it is not for us to elaborate a very profound analysis of the situation of the world, we have nevertheless been able to perceive the serious injustices which are building around the human world a network of domination, oppression and abuses which stifle freedom and which keep the greater part of humanity from sharing in the building up and enjoyment of a more just and more loving world.

4. At the same time we have noted the inmost stirring moving the world in its depths. There are facts constituting a contribution to the furthering of justice. In associations of people and among peoples themselves there is arising a new awareness which shakes them out of any fatalistic resignation and which spurs them on to liberate themselves and to be responsible for their own destiny. Movements among people are seen which express hope in a better world and a will to change whatever has become intolerable.

5. Listening to the cry of those who suffer violence and are oppressed by unjust systems and structures, and hearing the appeal of a world

that by its perversity contradicts the plan of its Creator, we have shared our awareness of the Church's vocation to be present in the heart of the world by proclaiming the Good News to the poor, freedom to the op-

> **"Good News to the poor . . .":**
>
> The phrases in this passage echo Luke 4:18, in which Jesus describes his mission in the world.

pressed, and joy to the afflicted. The hopes and forces which are moving the world in its very foundations are not foreign to the dynamism of the Gospel, which through the power of the Holy Spirit frees people from personal sin and from its consequences in social life.

6. The uncertainty of history and the painful convergences in the ascending path of the human community direct us to sacred history; there God has revealed himself to us, and made known to us, as it is brought progressively to realization, his plan of liberation and salvation which is once and for all fulfilled in the Paschal Mystery of Christ. Action on behalf of justice and participation in the transformation of the world fully appear to us as a constitutive dimension of the preaching of the Gospel, or, in other words, of the Church's mission for the redemption of the human race and its liberation from every oppressive situation.

The Gospel Message and the Mission of the Church

29. In the face of the present-day situation of the world, marked as it is by the grave sin of injustice, we recognize both our responsibility and our inability to overcome it by our own strength. Such a situation urges us to listen with a humble and open heart to the word of God, as he shows us new paths towards action in the cause of justice in the world.

30. In the Old Testament God reveals himself to us as the liberator of the oppressed and the defender of the poor, demanding from people faith in him and justice towards one's neighbor. It is only in the observance of the duties of justice that God is truly recognized as the liberator of the oppressed.

31. By his action and teaching Christ united in an indivisible way the relationship of people to God and the relationship of people to each other. Christ lived his life in the world as a total giving of himself to God for the

salvation and liberation of people. In his preaching he proclaimed the fatherhood of God towards all people and the intervention of God's justice on behalf of the needy and the oppressed (Lk 6:21–23). In this way he identified himself with his "least ones," as he stated: "As you did it to one of the least of these who are members of my family, you did it to me" (Mt 25:40).

32. From the beginning the Church has lived and understood the Death and Resurrection of Christ as a call by God to conversion in the faith of Christ and in love of one another, perfected in mutual help even to the point of a voluntary sharing of material goods.

33. Faith in Christ, the Son of God and the Redeemer, and love of neighbor constitute a fundamental theme of the writers of the New Testament. According to St. Paul, the whole of the Christian life is summed up in faith effecting that love and service of neighbor which involve the fulfillment of the demands of justice. The Christian lives under the interior law of liberty, which is a permanent call to us to turn away from self-sufficiency to confidence in God and from concern for self to a sincere love of neighbor. Thus takes place his genuine liberation and the gift of himself for the freedom of others.

34. According to the Christian message, therefore, our relationship to our neighbor is bound up with our relationship to God; our response to the love of God, saving us through Christ, is shown to be effective in his love and service of people. Christian love of neighbor and justice cannot be separated. For love implies an absolute demand for justice, namely a recognition of the dignity and rights of one's neighbor. Justice attains its inner fullness only in love. Because every person is truly a visible image of the invisible God and a sibling of Christ, the Christian finds in every person God himself and God's absolute demand for justice and love.

35. The present situation of the world, seen in the light of faith, calls us back to the very essence of the Christian message, creating in us a deep awareness of its true meaning and of its urgent demands. The mission of preaching the Gospel dictates at the present time that we should dedicate ourselves to the liberation of people even in their present existence in this world. For unless the Christian message of love and justice shows

its effectiveness through action in the cause of justice in the world, it will only with difficulty gain credibility with the people of our times.

36. The Church has received from Christ the mission of preaching the Gospel message, which contains a call to people to turn away from sin to the love of the Father, universal kinship and a consequent demand for justice in the world. This is the reason why the Church has the right, indeed the duty, to proclaim justice on the social, national and international level, and to denounce instances of injustice, when the fundamental rights of people and their very salvation demand it. The Church, indeed, is not alone responsible for justice in the world; however, she has a proper and specific responsibility which is identified with her mission of giving witness before the world of the need for love and justice contained in the Gospel message, a witness to be carried out in Church institutions themselves and in the lives of Christians.

37. Of itself it does not belong to the Church, insofar as she is a religious and hierarchical community, to offer concrete solutions in the social, economic and political spheres for justice in the world. Her mission involves defending and promoting the dignity and fundamental rights of the human person.

38. The members of the Church, as members of society, have the same right and duty to promote the common good as do other citizens. Christians ought to fulfil their temporal obligations with fidelity and competence. They should act as a leaven in the world, in their family, professional, social, cultural and political life. They must accept their responsibilities in this entire area under the influence of the Gospel and the teaching of the Church. In this way they testify to the power of the Holy Spirit through their action in the service of people in those things which are decisive for the existence and the future of humanity. While in such activities they generally act on their own initiative without involving the responsibility of the ecclesiastical hierarchy, in a sense they do involve the responsibility of the Church whose members they are.

leaven:

a substance that makes bread rise, such as yeast

ecclesiastical:

related to the Church

Excerpts from *Voice of the Voiceless: The Four Pastoral Letters and Other Statements*

by Archbishop Oscar Romero

The Church Continues the Work of Jesus

This is the message and the mission of Jesus that he, after he had risen, intended to go on preaching and living in the history of the world by means of his church. The church is the community of those who profess faith in Jesus Christ as the only Lord of history. It is a community of faith whose primary obligation, whose raison d'être, is to continue the life and work of Jesus.

> **raison d'être:**
> reason for being

To be church is to preserve in history, in and through the lives of men and women, the image of its Founder. The church principally exists for the evangelization of the human race. Yes, it is an institution; it is made up of persons, and it has forms and structures. But all that is for a much more basic reality: the exercise of its task of evangelization.

> **evangelization:**
> the proclamation of the Gospel

The church has always borne it in mind that in this task it has to go on proclaiming its faith in Jesus Christ, and that it has to continue, in the course of history, the work that Jesus carried out. When doing this it is the Body of Christ in history.

The Sphere of Its Rights and Duties

This well-defined purpose of the church also defines its duties and its rights—above all, the right and duty of following and loving in freedom its only Lord, Jesus Christ, known in faith. Then comes the right and duty of proclaiming the gospel without hindrance and of cooperating, in accord with its proper autonomy, in building up the kingdom of God among men and women in the way Christ wants it to be done today.

For that purpose it will use the means with which Christ himself has endowed it: preaching the word, administering the sacraments, above all celebrating the Eucharist—which will remind it, in an active, vital way, that it continues to be the Body of Christ. And it will also use those particular means that throw light on the question of what path is to be followed if the kingdom of God is to be realized. In other words: the church has to clarify faith in Jesus Christ and procedures for building up the kingdom of God in this world.

This is what the first Christians understood and lived out, those who "remained faithful to the teaching of the apostles, to the brotherhood, to the breaking of bread and to the prayers. . . . The faithful all lived together and owned everything in common; they sold their goods and possessions and shared out the proceeds among themselves according to what each one needed" (Acts 2:42,44).

Down through its history the church has carried out, with greater or lesser fidelity, that ideal of those first Christians in its following of Jesus. There have been times when the Church has more clearly been the Body of Christ. There have been times when it was not so clear—indeed, when it has been disfigured because it has accommodated itself to the world, seeking rather to be served by the world than itself to serve the world. But at other times its sincere wish has been to serve the world. On those occasions it has experienced rejection by the sinful world, just as its Founder did, even to the extent of persecution. That was the fate of the first Christians, of Peter and John before the courts, of Stephen the deacon, of Paul.

Like Jesus, the Church Proclaims the Kingdom of God

In Latin America, in El Salvador, the church, like Jesus, has to go on proclaiming the good news that the kingdom of God is at hand, especially for the great majority who, in worldly terms, have been estranged from it—the poor, the low-income classes, the marginalized. This does not mean that the church should neglect the other classes in society. It wants to serve them also, to enlighten them. It also needs their help in building up the kingdom. But the church should share Jesus' preference for those who have been used for others' interests and have not been in control of their own destinies.

The Church Denounces Sin and Calls to Conversion

The church, like Jesus, has to go on denouncing sin in our own day. It has to denounce the selfishness that is hidden in everyone's heart, the sin that dehumanizes persons, destroys families, and turns money, possessions, profit, and power into the ultimate ends for which persons strive. And, like anyone who has the smallest degree of foresight, the slightest capacity for analysis, the church has also to denounce what has rightly been called "structural sin": those social, economic, cultural, and political structures that effectively drive the majority of our people onto the margins of society. When the church hears the cry of the oppressed it cannot but denounce the social structures that give rise to and perpetuate the misery from which the cry arises.

But also like Christ, this denunciation by the church is not inspired by hatred or resentment. It looks to the conversion of heart of all men and women and to their salvation.

The Church Throws Light on the Kingdom of God

Jesus fulfilled his mission in a particular kind of world, in a particular sort of society. Like him, the church does not simply proclaim the kingdom of God in the abstract. It also has to promote the solutions that seem most likely to bring the kingdom into being, those that are most just. The church is well aware that to solve today's problems is a supremely difficult and complex task. It knows, furthermore, that in the last analysis it is not for it to put forward concrete solutions. And it knows that, in this world, it will never be possible fully to achieve the kingdom of God. But none of that exempts it from the pressing duty of publicizing and promoting the means that seem best able to help toward the partial realization of the kingdom.

In recent years everyone has come to know that the church has an interest in speaking out on matters concerning the ordered, rational, living together of human beings. A great number of documents have been issued by the church, from Leo XIII's encyclical *Rerum Novarum* (1891) to the recent exhortation *Evangelii Nuntiandi* by Paul VI (1976), which attempt to give guidance on what, at particular moments, have been the crucial problems facing society. The church has done so in order that, in denouncing sin and drawing attention to the paths to solutions, it may bring to the world the kingdom of God.

On March 5 of this year we Salvadoran bishops wrote, in fulfillment of this duty incumbent on the church, "Just as injustice takes concrete forms, so the promotion of justice must take concrete forms. It should come as a surprise to no one that the church encourages particular methods of achieving justice. Among those particular methods there will be some that are matters of opinion, and the church, too, will have to continue to learn which methods best bring about the ideal of the kingdom of God." And we added in our collective message of May 17, "The church believes that the world is called to be subject to Jesus Christ by way of a slow but sure establishment of the kingdom of God. . . . It believes in the kingdom of God as a progressive change from the world of sin to a world of love and justice, one that begins in this world but has its fulfillment in eternity."

Duty Arises from Loyalty to Christ

Only by fulfilling its mission in this way can the church be faithful to its own mystery, which is to be the Body of Christ in history. Only by living out its mission in this way, with the same spirit in which Jesus would have lived it out at this time and place, can it preserve its faith and give transcendent meaning to its message so that that message not be reduced to mere ideology or be manipulated by human selfishness or false traditionalism. It will move toward that final perfection of the kingdom of God in the world to come only if it strives to achieve, in the history of human society here on earth, the kingdom of truth and peace, of justice and love. . . .

ideology:

a system of beliefs or values that forms the basis of an economic or political philosophy

The Testimony of a Persecuted Church

calumnious:

having to do with calumny, false statements intended to hurt others

To the calumnious accusations that the church has been adulterating the Christian message has been added a series of events that amount to persecution of the church. An archdiocesan communiqué dated July 11 sums up the principal abuses to which the church has been subjected, priests expelled from, or prevented from entering, the country; calumnies; threats and assassinations; entire parishes deprived of their clergy; lay ministers of the word and catechists prevented from carrying out their duties; the Blessed Sacrament profaned in Aguilares. And all are aware of the lengthy, anonymous, and calumnious campaign being waged in the press against church-related persons and even against the church itself and its mission, as the church and its mission have been understood ever since Medellín.

> **Medellín:**
>
> a city in Colombia, and the site of the 1969 meeting of the Latin American bishops' conference, which issued a groundbreaking statement calling for the Church to act for social justice

But rather than simply detail such sad memories again, it seems to me more important to engage in a Christian reflection upon all these abuses now that some persons have been denying—despite all these outrages—that there is any persecution. They are saying that what has happened is in fact the church's fault, and blame it for the violent situation that exists in our country.

In the first place, no one should be surprised that the church is being persecuted precisely when it is being faithful to its mission. The Lord foretold it: "A servant is not greater than his master. If they persecuted me, they will persecute you too" (John 15:20). Christians have been subjected to persecution from the very beginning.

Why is the church persecuted? As I said earlier, the church is not an end in itself; it has a mission to pursue. Persecuting the church, therefore, does not consist only in attacking it directly, depriving it of privileges, or ignoring it juridically. The most serious persecution of the church is that which makes it impossible for it to carry out its mission, and which attacks those to whom its word of salvation is directed.

> **juridically:**
>
> legally

Even though the church is juridically recognized in our country, in recent months its mission has been attacked, and so have its priests and catechists who were trying to proclaim, and helping to bring into being, the kingdom of God. The Salvadoran people has been subjected to attack. Its human rights have been trodden underfoot—and protection of these rights falls under the church's responsibility. It is the church's belief that this persecution affects Christ himself: what touches any Christian touches Christ, because he is in personal union with all Christians—especially in anything that involves the poorest of society. "Saul, Saul, why are you persecuting me?" asks Christ of everyone who is persecuting his members. And at the last judgment Christ will reveal that "in so far as you did this to one of the least of these brothers of mine, you did it to me" (Matt. 25:40).

It is in this profound sense that the church can speak of persecution and can plead that this persecution cease. The church is persecuted when it is not allowed to proclaim the kingdom of God and all it entails in terms of justice, peace, love, and truth; when it is not allowed to denounce the sin of our land that engulfs people in wretchedness; when the rights of the people of El Salvador are not respected; when the number mounts steadily of those who have disappeared; been killed, or been calumniated.

It is also important to keep in mind that the church is persecuted because it wills to be in truth the church of Christ. The church is respected, praised, even granted privileges, so long as it preaches eternal salvation and does not involve itself in the real problems of our world. But if the church is faithful to its mission of denouncing the sin that brings misery to many, and if it proclaims its hope for a more just, humane world, then it is persecuted and calumniated, it is branded as subversive and communist.

During this time of persecution the church of the archdiocese has never returned evil for evil, it has never called for revenge or hatred. On the contrary, it has called for the conversion of those who persecute it, and, in our country's difficult problems, it has tried always to promote justice and avert worse evils.

The church hopes, with the help of God, to continue to witness with Christian courage in the midst of all difficulties. It knows that only by so doing will it win credibility for what it is proclaiming: that it is a church that has taken its place alongside those who suffer. It will not be frightened by the persecution that it undergoes, because persecution is a reaction to the church's fidelity to its divine Founder and to its solidarity with those most in need. . . .

For Reflection

1. Why is it essential that the Church act on behalf of justice? Summarize the reasons given in the readings.
2. What role does faith play in the decision of someone to risk his or her life for the sake of others? Draw from the readings, as well as the examples of Oscar Romero and Jean Donovan, in your answer.
3. What line or passage from these readings is most striking to you, and why?

Profile

Jean Donovan: Fulfilling the Mission of Christ in El Salvador

The people of La Libertad, El Salvador, called her Saint Jean the Playful, a title that fit her well. Back home in the United States, Jean Donovan was known for joking around, riding her motorcycle, and even pouring scotch whiskey over her breakfast cereal.

But Donovan's playfulness was balanced by a generous, compassionate spirit that drove her to seek a deeper meaning in life. When she heard about a mission project in El Salvador, she signed up as a lay volunteer—a move that meant quitting a good job at a major accounting firm. She wanted to go, she said, in order to get closer to God.

Donovan arrived in El Salvador in July 1979 to work with Caritas, a Catholic relief organization, in La Libertad. She and Ursuline Sister Dorothy Kazel distributed food to the poor, cared for wounded refugee children, and ran family education programs. Donovan regularly attended masses celebrated by Archbishop Romero and often baked chocolate chip cookies for him. She was at his funeral when government forces attacked, killing dozens of people. As the violence worsened, her two closest friends were murdered, and she began helping with the grim task of removing dead bodies from the streets for burial.

When she made a brief visit home to see her friends, family, and fiancé, many urged her to leave El Salvador. "I almost could except for the children, the poor bruised victims of this adult lunacy," she wrote a friend in late November 1980. "Who would care for them? Whose heart would be so staunch as to favor the reasonable thing in a sea of their tears and loneliness? Not mine, dear friend, not mine" (in Robert Ellsberg, *Blessed Among All Women,* p. 312).

Two weeks later, she and three companions—Sr. Dorothy Kazel and Maryknoll Sisters Maura Clarke and Ita Ford—were killed by a government death squad and dumped in a shallow grave.

The death of the four women stunned the Church in the United States, and moved many to oppose the U.S. policy supporting the Salvadoran military dictatorship. Nonetheless, the U.S. provided more than $6 billion in military aid to El Salvador, fueling a twelve-year civil war in which seventy-five thousand people died.

Donovan and her companions were not fearless. But their faith enabled them to overcome their fears, which freed them to love those most in need. In doing so, they became the body of Christ in the world.

Bartolomé de Las Casas

3

The Human Person and Human Rights

Introduction

One night in 1977, Patrick Sonnier and his brother abducted a teenage couple—David LeBlanc and Loretta Bourque—from a lover's lane near Saint Martinville, Louisiana. They raped Loretta and shot both her and David in the head. Patrick admitted his involvement in the crime, was convicted of murder, and was sentenced to death.

Does a person like Patrick Sonnier deserve to be respected as a human being? Sr. Helen Prejean answers that question with an unqualified "yes." She began a correspondence with Sonnier while he was on death row, and eventually became his spiritual advisor. After witnessing his execution in the electric chair, Prejean began speaking out against the death penalty. She wrote a book about her work with death row inmates, *Dead Man Walking*, that was made into an Academy Award–winning movie by the same name. Prejean may be more responsible than any other single person for the decline in public support for the death penalty in recent years.

Prejean believes that the dignity of a human person can never be taken away—not even when he or she commits a heartless crime, as Sonnier did. The Catholic Church supports her position. The Church teaches that in order to preserve the common good, violent criminals must be prevented from committing more crimes. But in modern societies, it is not necessary to kill someone in order to achieve that goal. Speaking in Saint Louis in 1999, Pope John Paul II said:

The dignity of human life must never be taken away, even in the case of someone who has done great evil. Modern society has the means of protecting itself, without definitively denying criminals the chance to reform. I renew the appeal I made most recently at Christmas for a consensus to end the death penalty, which is both cruel and unnecessary. (Homily at the Trans World Dome, no. 5)

Some people equate opposition to the death penalty with opposition to justice, or insensitivity to those affected by violent crimes. In fact, the Church teaches that the injustice caused by criminals must be repaired, and society has a special responsibility to care for those affected by crime. But the Church believes that retaliation—trying to hurt someone as much as she or he has hurt others—does not achieve these goals.

If it is difficult to understand why the Church would defend the dignity of someone like Patrick Sonnier, remember what *The Church in the Modern World* says about the source of human dignity: "Human dignity rests above all on the fact that humanity is called to communion with God" (no. 10). In other words, our dignity comes from God's love for us. That love is not limited by our sinful behavior; while we are free to turn away from God, God will never turn away from us. Therefore, human dignity can never be lost, and must always be respected.

To say that humans possess a natural dignity because of God's love for them implies that they have certain rights, those things that people need in order to live the kind of life God intends for them. Respecting human dignity, then, means also respecting human rights. The first major Catholic social teaching document on human rights was *Peace on Earth*, written by Pope John XXIII in 1963, partially in response to the Cuban missile crisis that brought the world to the brink of nuclear war. A major theme of the encyclical was that respect for human rights is the foundation of peace. Pope John Paul II returned to that theme in his 1999 message for the World Day of Peace, which is excerpted in this chapter.

Excerpts from the Message for the 1999 World Day of Peace

by Pope John Paul II

Respect for Human Rights: The Secret of True Peace

1. In my first Encyclical *Redemptor Hominis,* addressed almost twenty years ago to all men and women of good will, I stressed the importance of respect for human rights. Peace flourishes when these rights are fully respected, but when they are violated what comes is war, which causes other still graver violations.[1]

At the beginning of a new year, the last before the Great Jubilee, I would like to dwell once more on this crucially important theme with all of you, the men and women of every part of the world, with you, the political leaders and religious guides of peoples, with you, who love peace and wish to consolidate it in the world.

> **Great Jubilee:**
>
> The Church's celebration of the year 2000

Looking towards the World Day of Peace, let me state the conviction which I very much want to share with you: when the promotion of the dignity of the person is the guiding principle, and when the search for the common good is the overriding commitment, then solid and lasting foundations for building peace are laid. But when human rights are ignored or scorned, and when the pursuit of individual interests unjustly prevails over the common good, then the seeds of instability, rebellion and violence are inevitably sown.

Respect for Human Dignity, the Heritage of Humanity

2. The dignity of the human person is a transcendent value, always recognized as such by those who sincerely search for the truth. Indeed, the whole

> **transcendent:**
>
> beyond the material world

of human history should be interpreted in the light of this certainty. Every person, created in the image and likeness of God (cf. Gen 1:26–28) and therefore radically oriented towards the Creator, is constantly in relationship with those possessed of the same dignity. To promote the good of the individual is thus to serve the common good, which is that point where rights and duties converge and reinforce one another.

The history of our time has shown in a tragic way the danger which results from forgetting the truth about the human person. Before our eyes we have the results of ideologies such as Marxism, Nazism and Fascism, and also of myths like racial superiority, nationalism and ethnic exclusivism. No less pernicious, though not always as obvious, are the effects of materialistic consumerism, in which the exaltation of the individual and the selfish satisfaction of personal aspirations become the ultimate goal of life. In this outlook, the negative effects on others are considered completely irrelevant. Instead it must be said again that no affront to human dignity can be ignored, whatever its source, whatever actual form it takes and wherever it occurs.

The Universality and Indivisibility of Human Rights

3. The year 1998 has marked the fiftieth anniversary of the adoption of the Universal Declaration of Human Rights. The Declaration was intentionally linked to the United Nations Charter, since it shares a common inspiration. As its fundamental premise, it affirms that the recognition of the innate dignity of all members of the human family, as also the equality and inalienability of their rights, is the foundation of liberty, justice and peace in the world.[2] All the subsequent international documents on human rights declare this truth anew, recognizing and affirming that human rights stem from the inherent dignity and worth of the human person.[3]

Universal Declaration of Human Rights:

adopted by the United Nations in 1948, this document outlines basic human rights that apply to all people

The Universal Declaration is clear: it acknowledges the rights which it proclaims but does not confer them, since they are inherent in the human person and in human dignity. Consequently, no one can legitimately deprive another person, whoever they may be, of these rights, since this would do violence to their nature. All human beings, without exception, are equal in dignity. For the same reason, these rights apply to every stage of life and to every political, social, economic and cultural situation. Together they form a single whole, directed unambiguously towards the promotion of every aspect of the good of both the person and society.

Human rights are traditionally grouped into two broad categories, including on the one hand civil and political rights and on the other economic, social and cultural rights. Both categories, although to different degrees, are guaranteed by international agreements. All human rights are in fact closely connected, being the expression of different dimensions of a single subject, the human person. The integral promotion of every category of human rights is the true guarantee of full respect for each individual right.

Defence of the universality and indivisibility of human rights is essential for the construction of a peaceful society and for the overall development of individuals, peoples and nations. To affirm the universality and indivisibility of rights is not to exclude legitimate cultural and political differences in the exercise of individual rights, provided that in every case the levels set for the whole of humanity by the Universal Declaration are respected.

With these fundamental presuppositions clearly in mind, I would now like to identify certain specific rights which appear to be particularly exposed to more or less open violation today.

The Right to Life

4. The first of these is the basic right to life. Human life is sacred and inviolable from conception to its natural end. "Thou shalt not kill" is the divine

licit:

permitted

commandment which states the limit beyond which it is never licit to go. "The deliberate decision to deprive an innocent human being of life is always morally evil."[4]

The right to life is inviolable. This involves a positive choice, a choice for life. The development of a culture of this kind embraces all the circumstances of life and ensures the promotion of human dignity in every situation. A genuine culture of life, just as it guarantees to the unborn the right to come into the world, in the same way protects the newly born, especially girls, from the crime of infanticide. Equally, it assures the handicapped that they can fully develop their capacities, and ensures adequate care for the sick and the elderly.

Recent developments in the field of genetic engineering present a profoundly disquieting challenge. In order that scientific research in this area may be at the service of the person, it must be accompanied at every stage by careful ethical reflection, which will bring about adequate legal norms safeguarding the integrity of human life. Life can never be downgraded to the level of a thing.

To choose life involves rejecting every form of violence: the violence of poverty and hunger, which afflicts so many human beings; the violence of armed conflict; the violence of criminal trafficking in drugs and arms; the violence of mindless damage to the natural environment.[5] In every circumstance, the right to life must be promoted and safeguarded with appropriate legal and political guarantees, for no offence against the right to life, against the dignity of any single person, is ever unimportant.

Religious Freedom, the Heart of Human Rights

5. Religion expresses the deepest aspirations of the human person, shapes people's vision of the world and affects their relationships with others: basically it offers the answer to the question of the true meaning of life, both personal and communal. Religious freedom therefore constitutes the very heart of human rights. Its inviolability is such that individuals must be recognized as having the right even to change their religion, if their conscience so demands. People are obliged to follow their conscience in all circumstances and cannot be forced to act against it.[6] Precisely for this reason, no one can be compelled to accept a particular religion, whatever the circumstances or motives. . . .

The Right to Participate

6. All citizens have the right to participate in the life of their community: this is a conviction which is generally shared today. . . .

In the context of the international community, nations and peoples have the right to share in the decisions which often profoundly modify their way of life. . . .

A Particularly Serious Form of Discrimination

7. One of the most tragic forms of discrimination is the denial to ethnic groups and national minorities of the fundamental right to exist as such. This is done by suppressing them or brutally forcing them to move, or by attempting to weaken their ethnic identity to such an extent that they are no longer distinguishable. . . .

The Right to Self-Fulfillment

8. Every human being has innate abilities waiting to be developed. At stake here is the full actualization of one's own person and the appropriate insertion into one's social environment. In order that this may take place, it is necessary above all to provide adequate education to those who are just beginning their lives: their future success depends on this. . . .

actualization:

to make something real or actual

Another fundamental right, upon which depends the attainment of a decent level of living, is the right to work. Otherwise how can people obtain food, clothing, a home, health care and the many other necessities of life? . . .

Global Progress in Solidarity

9. The rapid advance towards the globalization of economic and financial systems also illustrates the urgent need to establish who is responsible for guaranteeing the global common good and the exercise of economic and social rights. The free market by itself cannot do this, because in fact there are many human needs which have no place in the market. "Even prior to the logic of a fair exchange of goods and the forms of justice appropriate to it, there exists something which is due to man because he is man, by reason of his lofty dignity."[7] . . .

Responsibility for the Environment

10. The promotion of human dignity is linked to the right to a healthy environment, since this right highlights the dynamics of the relationship between the individual and society. A body of international, regional and national norms on the environment is gradually giving juridic form to this

juridic:

relating to the law; legal

right. But juridic measures by themselves are not sufficient. The danger of serious damage to land and sea, and to the climate, flora and fauna, calls for a profound change in modern civilization's typical consumer lifestyle, particularly in the richer countries. . . .

The Right to Peace

11. In a sense, promoting the right to peace ensures respect for all other rights, since it encourages the building of a society in which structures of power give way to structures of cooperation, with a view to the common good. Recent history clearly shows the failure of recourse to violence as a means for resolving political and social problems. War destroys, it does not build up; it weakens the moral foundations of society and creates further divisions and long-lasting tensions. And yet the news continues to speak of wars and armed conflicts, and of their countless victims. How often have my Predecessors and I myself called for an end to these horrors! I shall continue to do so until it is understood that war is the failure of all true humanism.[8] . . .

A Culture of Human Rights, the Responsibility of All

12. It is not possible to discuss this topic more fully here. I would however like to emphasize that no human right is safe if we fail to commit ourselves to safeguarding all of them. When the violation of any fundamental human right is accepted without reaction, all other rights are placed at risk. It is therefore essential that there should be a global approach to the subject of human rights and a serious commitment to defend them. Only when a culture of human rights which respects different traditions becomes an integral part of humanity's moral patrimony shall we be able to look to the future with serene confidence. . . .

A Time of Decision, a Time of Hope

13. The new millennium is close at hand, and its approach has filled the hearts of many with hope for a more just and fraternal world. This is an aspiration which can, and indeed must, become a reality!

It is in this context that I now address you, dear Brothers and Sisters in Christ, who in all parts of the world take the Gospel as the pattern of your lives: become heralds of human dignity! Faith teaches us that every person has been created in the image and likeness of God. Even when man refuses it, the Heavenly Father's love remains steadfast; his is a love without limits. He sent his Son Jesus to redeem every individual, restoring each one's full human dignity.[9] With this in mind, how can we exclude anyone from our care? Rather, we must recognize Christ in the poorest and the most marginalized, those whom the Eucharist—which is communion in the body and blood of Christ given up for us—commits us to serve.[10] As the parable of the rich man, who will remain for ever without a name, and the poor man called Lazarus clearly shows, "in the stark contrast between the insensitive rich man and the poor in need of everything, God is on the latter's side."[11] We too must be on this same side. . . .

Endnotes

1. Cf. *Redemptor Hominis* (4 March 1979), 17: *AAS* 71 (1979), 296.

2. Cf. *Universal Declaration of Human Rights,* Preamble.

3. Cf. in particular the *Vienna Declaration* (25 June 1993), Preamble, 2.

4. John Paul II, Encyclical Letter *Evangelium Vitae* (25 March 1995), 57: *AAS* 87 (1995), 465.

5. Cf. *ibid.,* 10, *loc. cit.,* 412.

6. Cf. Second Vatican Ecumenical Council, Declaration on Religious Freedom *Dignitatis Humanae,* 3.

7. John Paul II, Encyclical Letter *Centesimus Annus* (1 May 1991), 34: *AAS* 83 (1991), 836.

8. Cf. in this regard the *Catechism of the Catholic Church,* 2307–2317.

9. Cf. John Paul II, Encyclical Letter *Redemptor Hominis* (4 March 1979), 13–14: *AAS* 71 (1979), 282–286.

10. Cf. *Catechism of the Catholic Church,* 1397.

11. John Paul II, Angelus Address, 27 September 1998, 1: *L'Osservatore Romano,* 28–29 September 1998, p. 5.

"With a Human Being Who's About to Be Killed"

by Sr. Helen Prejean

Sr. Helen Prejean, author of Dead Man Walking: An Eyewitness Account of the Death Penalty in the US, *has accompanied five men to execution, works with murder victims' families, and founded a group in New Orleans called Survive. This is an abridged version of her keynote address to the AFSC [American Friends Service Committee] Annual Public Gathering, November 6, 1999, in Philadelphia.*

I want to talk to you about the international movement to abolish the death penalty and the recent dramatic change within the Catholic church in that regard. It took me a long time to understand the connection between the Gospel message of Jesus Christ and justice. More than just being kind to individuals, it means to undo the system that kills and hurts people. Justice is a much harder thing to undertake than charity.

The discussion had come up in my community that we were not directly involved with poor people and justice. At first I really resisted that, but eventually I began to make my way into the neighborhoods where the poor people are. I began to realize how scared we are of poor people. Our society, our culture, builds up all these fearful images. When I did research for *Dead Man Walking,* I found that no matter how many peaceful things go on between people in Philadelphia today, the evening news will ferret out whatever violent acts happen, and show people those before they go to bed. It gives people an enhanced sense of danger, fearfulness of each other, "Don't go into that neighborhood, don't mix with those people." The more people get their knowledge of each other through television, the more trouble we're in.

There is something about being in the presence of people, real people, who are suffering from injustice or racism that ignites our souls with a passion; we can't walk away from it. That's what happened to me the minute I went into the first homeless shelter. Some people ask me, "Where do you get your energy?" It's not like you will energy! Energy comes to us because we get involved in something bigger than ourselves; our hearts have been moved by people's suffering, and we can't remain neutral. We say, "I don't know what I'm going to do, but I've got to do something. I've got to get involved in some way."

So I am in this climate in the St. Thomas Housing Projects. It was so simple and so casual when you think of it. "Hey Sister Helen, you want to be a pen pal to somebody on death row?" I just said, "Sure, yeah. Give me their name." I thought that all I was going to do was write a few letters, yeah. But then the person wrote back! I wasn't expecting all of this. The next thing I know I am accompanying this human being, Patrick Sonnier, walking with him, my hand on his shoulder. Unbelievable to me that this was happening.

St. Thomas Housing Projects:

a low-income housing project in New Orleans where Sister Helen lived and worked

In 1982, we hadn't executed anybody since the '60s. I never dreamed they were going to kill him in the end. I was telling him, "Patrick, when they do this thing, look at me. Look at my face." He had tried to protect me. We had known each other for two and a half years. "Look, Sister," he said, "you've been great and you've been with me. Just pray God holds up my legs, but you can't be there at the end. It could psychologically scar you." The love of him to me, trying to protect me, and then me knowing there was no way on God's earth that man was going to be killed and not have a loving face to look at. It's not like it was virtue, it's not like it was courage, it was just simply what you or anyone would do when you're with a human being who's about to be killed.

That was a transforming point in my life. You cannot be there behind a Plexiglas screen and see the scripted death of a human being, see him being led into the room, strapped into a chair, a mask put over his face, and being killed in front of your eyes—you cannot be there and be in the presence of that kind of blinding light, and walk out and say, "I'm not going to do this any more." Something ignited in my own soul, and I guess the basic thing was that I realized that I was a witness. I had seen the death penalty close up. I got conscripted.

I remember saying to myself, when I came out of that execution chamber, "If the American people could see this, they wouldn't choose this. They don't know what's going on." This was a practice of torture, this was wrong, it's against our whole moral tradition.

An important part of spirituality is that it helps us dive deep to that point of unity where we are no longer us and them, with the victims on one side and the people receiving the death penalty on the other.

The death penalty is not about redressing wrongs, restoring life. For politicians, it's a symbol of how tough they're going to be on crime, that they're doing something substantive. When I came out of that execution chamber, I began to learn about the death penalty. Are we talking about an anti-crime measure when there are about 17,000 capital cases in this country and 1.5% of them are going to be chosen for death, and even fewer than that are going to be executed?

Look at New York. The death penalty was a key part of George Pataki's campaign. Four years later: 488 homicide cases, possible capital cases; out of those, 38 are chosen for the death penalty. Out of those, five people have death sentences, and that's $68 million later. Then, in his State of the Union address last year, George Pataki claimed that the murder rate was going down in New York because you've got the death penalty. Of course. The murder rate has gone down in Boston, it's gone down in your area, it's going down in states that don't have the death penalty. The violence rate has been going down.

The only way to change things is to change consciousness by having people dialogue. I've been very heartened to see the film's tremendous impact. I spoke at the University of North Carolina. They showed the film twice earlier in the week, and all the freshmen have been assigned the book for summer reading. When I get onto the campus, the soil is tilled! Seventeen hundred freshmen and the faculty have read the book. There's a buzz on the campus about the death penalty. It's like you go in, you take them through it, you point to the alternative and you say, "We don't have to do this anymore." At the end of the talk they stand up and applaud!

Did you hear that when Clinton went to Oslo there was a public demonstration on the streets, led mostly by young people, calling the United States to account for the death penalty, for trying to police the world?

The Council of Europe has as one of its requirements for joining that a country can't have the death penalty. Boris Yeltsin, this past year, commuted all the sentences of people on death row in Russia. In 1900, only four countries in the world had abolition. Now they're estimating that 100 to 105 have, and there is a fierce struggle going on right now in the UN because they're going to introduce the resolution for a worldwide moratorium on the death penalty, and the United States is going ballistic behind the scenes, twisting arms. They don't want that to get to the floor. They're trying to kill it by amendments. In Geneva at the UN Commission on Human Rights, the majority of countries, including Russia and Eastern Europe, were saying, "Moratorium, moratorium." The United States voted with China, Iran, and Iraq.

Gandhi said that oppressors stop oppressing usually not for high, lofty, moral reasons but because it gets too costly. We can see it with the United States and the UN.

Moral disequilibrium is the presage to change. The United States, like any country, wants to have pride, and we stand before the world as a symbol of democracy and some of the best values on this earth. For Clinton to be brokering peace in the Middle East and have students shouting, as he gets out of the car, "What about the death penalty, Mr. Clinton?" to be accosted by your peers and your allies, that's costly. I'm not saying it's going to change overnight, but when the United States stands up before the world to call for human rights, they know they've got a vulnerable flank. That is part of the movement toward peace.

One of the reasons we have 82 innocent people who've come off of death row is not because of the courts' justice. It's because individual citizens got interested in their cases, and brought them to light. Anthony Porter was about to be executed by Illinois. He got a stay of execution because two journalism students from Northwestern were assigned by their professor to look into the case. They went into town and started talking to people. In two weeks they'd unraveled the whole bloomin' thing! The people were saying, "Oh, we know who the real murderer is." The key eyewitness recants and blump, blump, blump, the whole thing comes apart, and they've got to let Anthony Porter go as the twelfth person that Illinois freed.

A member of the Italian Parliament by the name of Luciano Nari sees a little clip in the paper. "Hey, here's this man Joseph O'Dell in Virginia. He's asking for a DNA test and they won't let him have it." He calls Washington, and hooks up with a certain Laurie Errs. The Italian Parliament sends a delegation to visit Joseph O'Dell. They ask to see the governor of Virginia. He doesn't want to see this bunch of Italians. They go back and start spreading the word about Joseph O'Dell. If you go to Italy today and say, "Joseph O'Dell," they know him, like Princess Di! They started doing public demonstrations in St. Peter's Square, in front of the Pope's window.

I'm minding my own business. I never heard of Joseph O'Dell, and I get a phone call from Laurie Errs asking me to speak at a press conference about Joseph's case. So I go to Richmond and now I'm involved with Joseph O'Dell. The next thing you know the Mayor of Palermo, who will forever live in a bullet-proof car with guards around him because he took on the Mafia, hears about Joseph O'Dell. He comes over and they let him into the prison. He tells Joseph, "If they kill you, we will make you an honorary citizen of Palermo and we will bury you there."

Now sacks of mail are beginning to come to Joseph O'Dell from the Italian people. The governor gets 10,000 faxes and phone calls. It took four people just to field the calls from the Italians. He blew them all off, including the Pope and Mother Teresa. "Hey, hey, what do I care about the Italians? We're doing justice here in Virginia." In the end they killed Joseph O'Dell. There's a slab on his grave in Palermo that says, "Joseph O'Dell, killed by the merciless and unjust justice system in Virginia."

I wrote a letter to the Pope telling him about an experience that Joseph had had in August when he came close to death. He had watched three people go to the shower right outside that cell, put on the white jumpsuit and go into the execution chamber. One of them was his good friend. He was next, and at the last minute they said, "You've got a stay of execution, go back to your cell." He was crying, saying, "They almost killed me. They killed my friend." I wrote, "Your Holiness, when we talk about the dignity of the human person, how are we going to take the torture out of the death penalty? If you're torturing somebody, how can you say we're upholding their dignity?"

I told him that because his encyclical said that the death penalty should be rare or non-existent, but in cases of absolute necessity the state could do it. The Catholic District Attorney in New Orleans, Harry Connick Sr., seized on this, saying, "We can't get enough death penalties in Louisiana; it's always an absolute necessity." I said, "Your words are being quoted for death and we've got to take those words out. All human beings have the right to life, guilty people, too. Most of the pro-life people I meet are pro–innocent life, but they're sure not pro–guilty life. Is there a difference? Did Jesus come only to the innocent, or is there a way that we can stand in the dignity of all human life, even those among us who have done terrible crimes?"

The letter was delivered to him on January 22nd. One week later, the Vatican announced, "There's going to be a change in the Catechism." They cut out the part that said, "For grievous or heinous crimes the state can execute," which is what every legislator and every George Pataki and everybody who's for the death penalty says. And so we have a coming together of religion (in its good and truest and deepest sense) and human rights. This is what's going to bring us into the next millennium. It sets our agenda for the next millennium and is the source of life for the next millennium, and everybody sitting in this room today is part of that. There's part of it in every effort we make for life and the dignity of life, every effort we make for restorative justice instead of for punitive justice, every effort we make to connect people together as neighbors. The only way we can kill each other is when we're disconnected, and we're allowed to say, "Oh, they're not human the way we're human, and it's okay to kill them."

restorative and punitive justice:

Restorative justice attempts to restore right relationships and promote healing, while punitive justice focuses on punishing offenders.

I think the death penalty simply epitomizes the three deepest wounds we have in our society. One is the racism that riddles it. Mostly it's when white people get killed that the death penalty is even sought. Racism is in this thing inside and out. Our penchant for choosing the poor to pay the ultimate price and to suffer the harshest punishments, to make them the scapegoats—that's another wound. The third is our penchant for trying to solve our social problems with military solutions. The death penalty is one more military solution: target an enemy, dehumanize the enemy, and kill the enemy. The book of Deuteronomy says, "Look, I set before you death and life. Choose life."

For Reflection

1. The Pope says human rights are universal and indivisible: "When the violation of any fundamental human right is accepted without reaction, all other rights are placed at risk" (Message for the 1999 World Day of Peace, no. 12). Choose one of the human rights mentioned by the Pope, and explain how violating that right would put other rights at risk.
2. Imagine for a moment that society lived according to the ideas proposed by Sr. Helen Prejean and Pope John Paul II. What might people have done differently to restore justice following the murders of David and Loretta? Describe the situation as specifically as possible, using the words of the Pope or Sister Prejean to support your ideas.
3. What statement or idea in these readings most challenges your current views or ways of thinking, and why?

Profile

Bartolomé de Las Casas: Defender of Human Rights

The Spaniards who conquered the Americas in the early sixteenth century had little regard for the dignity or rights of the native population. In fact, most Spanish did not hesitate to kill and enslave the Indians, who they regarded as an inferior race.

Bartolomé de Las Casas (1484–1566) was horrified by the Spaniards' harsh treatment of the natives when he first came to the Americas as a young deacon. That did not stop him from managing his family's property there, including Indian slaves—a situation that made him increasingly uncomfortable as he witnessed more atrocities against the Indians. The preaching of a small group of Dominican priests influenced him as well. Las Casas recorded a sermon in which one of the Dominicans, Antonio de Montesinos, warned the Spanish that their treatment of the Indians was endangering their very souls:

> Tell me, by what right or justice do you hold these Indians in such a cruel and horrible servitude? . . . Why do you keep them so oppressed and exhausted, without giving them enough to eat or

curing them of the sicknesses they incur from the excessive labor you give them. . . ? Are these not men? Do they not have rational souls? Are you not bound to love them as you love yourselves? (George Sanderlin, ed., *Witness*, p. 67)

Eventually Las Casas (who had become a priest) came to see in the Indians not only human dignity, but in their suffering, the crucified Christ. He renounced his ownership of Indians and joined the Dominicans in defending the native population, despite open hostility from other Spaniards. In his numerous books and letters, Las Casas describes the art, culture, religion, and civic institutions of the Indians as a way of emphasizing their inherent dignity. He vividly describes the Indians' mistreatment in works like *A Short Account of the Destruction of the Indies*. As a missionary, he sought to convert the native people to Christianity by treating them with kindness and respect, and by actually teaching them about the faith—an unusual approach at a time when too many Spaniards forced the Indians to either convert or be killed. And Las Casas frequently returned to Spain to personally request the king's protection of the Indians. Although the Spanish king passed laws forbidding the enslavement of the Indians, the laws were mostly ignored, and were eventually repealed.

Despite overwhelming opposition, Las Casas devoted more than fifty years of his life to defending the human rights and dignity of the native population. For that reason, he remains a model for all who work against great odds to defend the rights of the oppressed and marginalized today.

Eileen Egan

4

Principles of the Church's Social Doctrine

Introduction

"Where there is no prophecy, the people cast off restraint," says the Book of Proverbs (29:18). The U.S. Catholic bishops adapt this verse in their 1988 document *Sharing Catholic Social Teaching: Challenges and Directions* to underscore the point that if human society is to flourish, it needs a guiding vision— a picture of what society might look like if it lived according to God's word.

At the time the Book of Proverbs was written, prophets provided the people with this vision. Today, Catholics (along with other people) find a prophetic vision in the Church's social teaching. That teaching provides principles by which Christians might fully live out the Gospel in the modern world, with all its complexities and challenges. The U.S. Catholic bishops outline some of those principles, along with seven broad themes of Catholic social teaching in *Sharing Catholic Social Teaching:* the life and dignity of the human person, participation in family and social life, rights and responsibilities, the option for the poor and vulnerable, the dignity of work and the rights of workers, solidarity, and care for God's creation. As different as all these themes may seem to be, in reality they all work interdependently to protect and promote the dignity of human life. Together they form what Catholic peace activist Eileen Egan calls a "seamless garment." Just as the soldiers at the Crucifixion could not divide Jesus's tunic without destroying it (see John 19:23), human dignity is threatened when the justice principles outlined in Catholic social teaching are "divided" by following some and ignoring others.

With four thousand field staff working to relieve human suffering in ninety-nine countries around the world, the people at Catholic Relief Services (CRS) have personal experience with the power of Catholic social teaching to make a real difference in the world. They also know all too well the truth of the biblical saying, "Without a vision, the people perish." In 1994, tensions between two rival ethnic groups in the African country of Rwanda exploded; neighbor slaughtered neighbor, killing a million people in one hundred days.

The violence directly affected CRS staff members working in Rwanda, many of whom lost friends, relatives, and colleagues. But it also prompted the entire organization to re-evaluate the way it approached its work, as CRS president Ken Hackett explained in a 2005 speech at Seattle University: "After much reflection, we resolved to address not just the symptoms of crises, but also the systems and structures that underlie the continued oppression and poverty so many in the developing world face," Hackett said. "And we rediscovered a jewel in our religious tradition that has enabled us to effectively do this: Catholic social teaching" ("Building Solidarity," Catholic Relief Sevices Web site).

Hackett's insight gets at the real meaning and importance of justice. Peter Maurin, co-founder of the Catholic Worker movement, often said that Christians should strive to create a society in which it is easier for people to be good. Being good to one another—what we call charity—is the foundation of justice. But justice goes beyond charity, beyond "making right" the basic relationships that shape society, so that goodness can flourish.

Catholic social teaching provides the prophetic vision necessary to create such a society. As you read about it, try to imagine what that vision might look like in your own world.

Excerpts from *Sharing Catholic Social Teaching: Challenges and Directions*

by the United States Conference of Catholic Bishops

Introduction

Our community of faith is blessed with many gifts. Two of the most vital are our remarkable commitment to Catholic education and catechesis in all its forms and our rich tradition of Catholic social teaching. As we look to a new millennium, there is an urgent need to bring these two gifts together in a strengthened commitment to sharing our social teaching at every level of Catholic education and faith formation.

Catholic social teaching is a central and essential element of our faith. Its roots are in the Hebrew prophets who announced God's special love for the poor and called God's people to a covenant of love and justice. It is a teaching founded on the life and words of Jesus Christ, who came "to bring glad tidings to the poor . . . liberty to captives . . . recovery of sight to the blind" (Lk 4:18–19), and who identified himself with "the least of these," the hungry and the stranger (cf. Mt 25:45). Catholic social teaching is built on a commitment to the poor. This commitment arises from our experiences of Christ in the Eucharist. As the *Catechism of the Catholic Church* explains, "To receive in truth the Body and Blood of Christ given up for us, we must recognize Christ in the poorest, his brethren" (no. 1397).

Catholic social teaching emerges from the truth of what God has revealed to us about himself. We believe in the triune God whose very nature is communal and social. God the Father sends his only Son Jesus Christ and shares the Holy Spirit as his gift of love. God reveals himself to us as one who is not alone, but rather as one who is relational, one who is Trinity. Therefore, we who are made in God's image share this communal, social nature. We are called to reach out and to build relationships of love and justice.

Catholic social teaching is based on and inseparable from our understanding of human life and human dignity. Every human being is created in the image of God and redeemed by Jesus Christ, and therefore is invaluable and worthy of respect as a member of the human family. Every person, from the moment of conception to natural death, has inherent dignity and a right to life consistent with that dignity. Human dignity comes from God, not from any human quality or accomplishment.

Our commitment to the Catholic social mission must be rooted in and strengthened by our spiritual lives. In our relationship with God we experience the conversion of heart that is necessary to truly love one another as God has loved us. . . .

Catholic Social Teaching: Major Themes

The Church's social teaching is a rich treasure of wisdom about building a just society and living lives of holiness amidst the challenges of modern society. It offers moral principles and coherent values that are badly needed in our time. In this time of widespread violence and diminished respect for human life and dignity in our country and around the world, the Gospel of life and the biblical call to justice need to be proclaimed and shared with new clarity, urgency, and energy.

Modern Catholic social teaching has been articulated through a tradition of papal, conciliar, and episcopal documents that explore and express the social demands of our faith. The depth and richness of this tradition

conciliar:

related to a Church council

can be understood best through a direct reading of these documents, many of which are cited in the Report of the Content Subgroup. In these brief reflections, we wish to highlight several of the key themes that are at the heart of our Catholic social tradition. We hope they will serve as a

episcopal:

related to the bishop

starting point for those interested in exploring the Catholic social tradition more fully.

Life and Dignity of the Human Person

In a world warped by materialism and declining respect for human life, the Catholic Church proclaims that human life is sacred and that the dignity of the human person is the foundation of a moral vision for society. Our belief in the sanctity of human life and the inherent dignity of the human person is the foundation of all the principles of our social teaching. In our society, human life is under direct attack from abortion and assisted suicide. The value of human life is being threatened by increasing use of the death penalty. The dignity of life is undermined when the creation of human life is reduced to the manufacture of a product, as in human cloning or proposals for genetic engineering to create "perfect" human beings. We believe that every person is precious, that people are more important than things, and that the measure of every institution is whether it threatens or enhances the life and dignity of the human person.

Call to Family, Community, and Participation

In a global culture driven by excessive individualism, our tradition proclaims that the person is not only sacred but also social. How we organize our society—in economics and politics, in law and policy—directly affects human dignity and the capacity of individuals to grow in community. The family is the central social institution that must be supported and strengthened, not undermined. While our society often exalts individualism, the Catholic tradition teaches that human beings grow and achieve fulfillment in community. We believe people have a right and a duty to participate in society, seeking together the common good and well-being of all, especially the poor and

common good: the overall state of society that enables all people to more easily fulfill their human dignity

vulnerable. Our Church teaches that the role of government and other institutions is to protect human life and human dignity and promote the common good.

Rights and Responsibilities

In a world where some speak mostly of "rights" and others mostly of "responsibilities," the Catholic tradition teaches that human dignity can be protected and a healthy community can be achieved only if human rights are protected and responsibilities are met. Therefore, every person has a fundamental right to life and a right to those things required for human decency. Corresponding to these rights are duties and responsibilities—to one another, to our families, and to the larger society. While public debate in our nation is often divided between those who focus on personal responsibility and those who focus on social responsibilities, our tradition insists that both are necessary.

Option for the Poor and Vulnerable

In a world characterized by growing prosperity for some and pervasive poverty for others, Catholic teaching proclaims that a basic moral test is how our most vulnerable members are faring. In a society marred by deepening divisions between rich and poor, our tradition recalls the story of the Last Judgment (Mt 25:31–46) and instructs us to put the needs of the poor and vulnerable first.

The Dignity of Work and the Rights of Workers

In a marketplace where too often the quarterly bottom line takes precedence over the rights of workers, we believe that the economy must serve people, not the other way around. Work is more than a way to make a living; it is a form of continuing participation in God's creation. If the dignity of work is to be protected, then the basic rights of workers must be respected—the right to productive work, to decent and fair wages, to organize and join unions, to private property, and to economic initiative. Respecting these rights promotes an economy that protects human life, defends human rights, and advances the well-being of all.

Solidarity

Our culture is tempted to turn inward, becoming indifferent and sometimes isolationist in the face of international responsibilities. Catholic social teaching proclaims that we are our brothers' and sisters' keepers, wherever they live. We are one human family, whatever our national, racial, ethnic, economic, and ideological differences. Learning to practice the virtue of solidarity means learning that "loving our neighbor" has global dimensions in an interdependent world. This virtue is described by John Paul II as "a firm and persevering determination to commit oneself to the common good; that is to say to the good of all and of each individual, because we are all really responsible for all" (*Sollicitudo Rei Socialis*, no. 38).

Care for God's Creation

On a planet conflicted over environmental issues, the Catholic tradition insists that we show our respect for the Creator by our stewardship of creation. Care for the earth is not just an Earth Day slogan, it is a requirement of our faith. We are called to protect people and the planet, living our faith in relationship with all of God's creation. This environmental challenge has fundamental moral and ethical dimensions that cannot be ignored.

This teaching is a complex and nuanced tradition with many other important elements. Principles like "subsidiarity" and the "common good" outline the advantages and limitations of markets, the responsibilities and limits of government, and the essential roles of voluntary associations. These and other key principles are outlined in greater detail in the *Catechism* and in the Report of the Content Subgroup. These principles build on the foundation of Catholic social teaching: the

subsidiarity:

a principle of social justice that states that the function of larger social units should be limited to supporting or assisting smaller social units in carrying out their social responsibilities

dignity of human life. This central Catholic principle requires that we measure every policy, every institution, and every action by whether it protects human life and enhances human dignity, especially for the poor and vulnerable.

These moral values and others outlined in various papal and episcopal documents are part of a systematic moral framework and a precious intellectual heritage that we call Catholic social teaching. The Scriptures say, "Without a vision the people perish" (Prv 29:18). As Catholics, we have an inspiring vision in our social teaching. In a world that hungers for a sense of meaning and moral direction, this teaching offers ethical criteria for action. In a society of rapid change and often confused moral values, this teaching offers consistent moral guidance for the future. For Catholics, this social teaching is a central part of our identity. In the words of John Paul II, it is "genuine doctrine" (*Centesimus Annus*, no. 5).

There will be legitimate differences and debate over how these challenging moral principles are applied in concrete situations. Differing prudential judgments on specifics cannot be allowed, however, to obscure the need for every Catholic to know and apply these principles in family, economic, and community life. . . .

Excerpts from "Building Solidarity: From Rwanda to the Asian Tsunami"

by Ken Hackett

A New Paradigm

. . . In 1994, we had been working in Rwanda, a Catholic country, since before independence in the 1960s. We knew there were ethnic tensions between the Hutus and the Tutsis. But we concluded that addressing them was not a part of our mandate.

Hutus and Tutsis: different ethnic groups in Rwanda

Then we experienced the genocide—upwards of a million people murdered over a scant three months. It deeply affected us. Our CRS staff lost friends, colleagues and family members. And we learned that all the good work we had been doing—the silos and schools we built, the children we fed, the farms we planted—was not enough.

genocide: the attempt to destroy a particular racial, ethnic, religious, or national population

We realized that we had not addressed the justice issues relating to the structures that perpetuated societal imbalances in Rwanda. After much reflection, we resolved to address not just the symptoms of crises, but also the systems and structures that underlie the continued oppression and poverty so many in the developing world face. We began incorporating a justice-centered focus in all our programming. And we rediscovered a jewel in our religious tradition that has enabled us to effectively do this: Catholic Social Teaching.

Catholic Social Teaching calls people to solidarity, to balance relationships in society and among ourselves. It places the dignity of the human person at the center of all we do. It upholds the principle of subsidiarity: that higher levels of an organization like CRS should

tsunami:

a devastating wave of water. Here, Hackett is referring to the tsunami that struck parts of Asia on December 26, 2004, killing more than 229,000 people and displacing millions more.

not perform any function or duty that could be better handled at a more local level, by people who better know the cultural, social and political context than we do.

With Catholic Social Teaching as our guide, we adopted a new paradigm that we call the "Justice Lens." We re-examined everything we did—our programs, our policies, how we related to the people we serve, how we related to the U.S. Catholic community, how we related to one another as fellow employees of CRS—and evaluated them in terms of whether they help to build a culture of justice, peace and reconciliation.

Even in a disaster like the tsunami, our emergency response was guided by the Justice Lens. Here are five perspectives on how we're doing this:

1. Justice affects how we respond to a disaster. As we saw in the Rwandan situation, interventions must establish right relations in society. After the tsunami, there was a terrific response by the U.S. government. In a show of humanitarian force, the aircraft carrier U.S.S. Abraham Lincoln was diverted from training exercises in Hong Kong and arrived New Year's Day off the coast of Indonesia. Over the next month, the carrier served as a base of operations for dozens of daily helicopter flights that brought badly needed supplies to remote villages. The operation was welcomed, but was also greeted with some ambivalence. It was literally an invasion—although a benevolent invasion. The presence of such a Western power in a society with a very different religious, cultural and social outlook caused unease. The U.S. wisely decided to wrap up its effort and the Abraham Lincoln was gone by Feb. 4.

That response was important. It was necessary. And it helped people. But it was not particularly mindful of what was going on in the communities. Whose homes were destroyed, who survived and left and who had to stay behind. For us, relationships count. Providing assistance can foster harmonious relations or re-enforce imbalances, inequalities in societies. We come for the long term. And we work with local people and organizations, soliciting their input and quickly putting them in charge of their own destinies. We also assess the possible negative impact that our aid might bring—it could reinforce inequalities in a community, or it could distort the local economy. And we try to identify opportunities for building just and peaceful relationships among groups in the places we serve.

2. Justice means that it's important to consider not just WHAT relief is delivered, but HOW it is delivered. Because Catholic Social Teaching stresses the importance of upholding the dignity of the human person, we want to avoid making the people we serve become dependent on the aid we deliver.

Therefore, relief isn't just a matter of handing out food and building houses. Our relief strategy involves a continuum of services that address the social, cultural and economic factors that will help people to restore their lives and livelihoods.

Our approach to shelter is a good example of this approach. We try to integrate the building of a home with a number of programs that will help them become self-sufficient.

First of all, shelter is not just a product, but it is a family's home, a social meeting place, it can be an economic benefit and a place where ancestors are buried.

All this goes into deciding where a house should be built and what materials should be used. There are land issues to settle in the countries hit by the tsunami. Many families will not be allowed to rebuild in a certain buffer zone along the coastline. And the availability of local building materials and the impact of using them on the local economy must also be considered. The communities affected, as well as our local partners, have a voice in addressing all of these issues.

The actual building of the house also offers us an opportunity. Offering cash or food for work in building the houses provides employment that can help restart the local economy. And the house becomes less of a handout if a family can help in its construction.

3. Justice calls us to address the whole person as well as material loss. In our experience, we have found that one of the greatest effects of a disaster is the psychological trauma it causes survivors. This has been particularly true of the tsunami.

Catholic Social Teaching emphasizes the importance of maintaining and building up the dignity of the human person—dignity that is oftentimes a casualty in a disaster. That is why treating psychological trauma has been an important part of our response, and it will continue to be a key part of our long-term recovery programs.

In the first days after the tsunami, the lead psychologist with the Maryland State Police, Dr. Michael Finegan, volunteered his services. We flew him to Galle, a city on Sri Lanka's southern tip that suffered more than 4,200 fatalities. While he was there, Dr. Finegan trained hundreds of community leaders, health care workers, religious leaders and teachers in how to recognize and deal with psychological trauma.

4. Justice leads us to work in solidarity with local partners and to encourage local solutions. We work and respect the local agencies who either are already our partners in previous development work, or who will become our partners in addressing this latest crisis. We can't do the work all by ourselves, nor should we.

After the tsunami, we were able to respond extremely quickly in places where we already have programs. This gives us an advantage because we understand the local situation; we have existing relationships with governments and religious and civic organizations; and we have personnel already in place or nearby. In the case of India, where we have long-established relationships with Catholic organizations, relief work started within hours after the tsunami. This network of partners increases our effectiveness and ensures that our work will be carried on after we leave.

5. Justice compels us to reach out to those here in the U.S. who responded with prayers and financial contributions. After the first reports of the massive death, there was a country-wide outpouring from the American public like I've never seen in my three-decade career in humanitarian work.

The challenge now for us is to continue to engage those people who opened their hearts to the people of India, Indonesia, Sri Lanka and Thailand. Again, the answer is solidarity. One example is an effort by the Diocese of Metuchen, NJ, which has committed to help in an extended recovery effort in the Thanjuvar Diocese in India. Metuchen is the first U.S. diocese to commit to a long-term relationship for recovery and restoration in the tsunami-ravaged region.

It is expected that the Metuchen/Thanjuvar effort will involve two phases over the next 18 to 24 months. The first is an intermediate resettlement phase that will happen in the next few months. The second is a livelihood restoration phase. Metuchen will work with CRS India and Caritas India (sort of like the local Catholic Charities) in a focus on orphan care, housing and the restoration of the local fishing industry.

This is the true meaning of solidarity—not just writing a check, but concrete action on behalf of the suffering.

Silent Tsunamis

The tsunami is taking up much of our attention but it is not the only matter that we're focused on. We were facing other crises before Dec. 26—and new ones have emerged since then. We call them our silent tsunamis.

The biggest crisis we're addressing—and will continue to address for years to come—is the tragedy of the HIV/AIDS pandemic, particularly in Africa. In the last 20 years, HIV and AIDS have infected more than 42 million people, and nearly three-quarters of them live in Africa. CRS started our first HIV and AIDS programs in 1989 in Masaka, Uganda. We now have HIV/AIDS programs in nearly 50 countries across Africa and in the hardest-hit areas of Asia, Europe and Latin America. This year, CRS will directly help nearly 2 million people with HIV/AIDS.

One ray of hope in fighting this pandemic is the use of antiretroviral drugs, a combination of medicines that helps reverse the progression of HIV in the body. Last year, as the result of an unprecedented grant by the U.S. government, CRS became the lead agency in a five-organization consortium called AIDSRelief to expand the delivery of antiretroviral treatment to people infected with HIV in Africa, the Caribbean and Latin America. The grant is expected to total $335 million over five years.

The treatment is already showing results that one could only call miraculous. There is the story of Doreen Otieno, a flower farmer in Kenya who could not afford the life-saving antiretroviral treatment from private or Government health services on the $43 she earned each month. Then, she began receiving the antiretroviral treatment through the AIDSRelief-supported Nazareth Hospital in Limuru, Kenya. Before, her body was wracked with opportunistic diseases like meningitis and she was unable to work. After five months on the treatment, she gained 18 pounds and is strong enough to work again at the flower farm. But the biggest effect, she said, has been in the lives of her children, now 14 and 10 years old. She told us: "Now, the money I used to spend on hospitals is no longer taken from my salary. So now my children are back in school." . . .

Conclusion

Solidarity is a difficult concept to embrace in this post–Sept. 11 era. We live in a fragmented world. Our country is divided into blue states and red states. In the war on terror, the world is divided into ally and enemy.

But over and over again, we are reminded that we are one human family: the tenacity of a woman like Doreen Otieno, battling AIDS and trying to live for her children; the dignity of the displaced in Sudan, outraged at the violation of their human rights; the gratitude and hope of singing children amid the ruins in Indonesia. These are reminders that our brothers and sisters are in need, and now more than ever, what is needed is solidarity.

We believe that solidarity can transform the world; we believe that it is the responsibility of all of us to ensure that it does; and we know that with God's mercy, it will.

For Reflection

1. Think of a social justice issue that concerns you, either locally or globally. Briefly describe the issue in a paragraph or two. Then write another paragraph or two describing how one or more principles of Catholic social teaching might be applied to the issue.
2. Ken Hackett emphasizes the need to be careful about how assistance is provided to those in need. What insights from his speech might be useful for someone addressing the social justice issue you described in question 1, and why?
3. In your opinion, what is the most important idea in these readings? Support your answer with evidence from the readings.

Profile

Eileen Egan: Prophet of Peace

Besides its social teaching, the Church also offers the world a prophetic vision through those rare individuals who help others imagine new ways of living the Gospel. One such person is Eileen Egan, a journalist who devoted her life to the cause of peace.

After witnessing the horrors of war firsthand as a freelance journalist covering World War II, Egan was moved to join the United States Catholic bishops' newly created War Relief Services organization in 1943. She spent more than forty years working as a project coordinator for the organization, which was later renamed Catholic Relief Services. Her work took her to every corner of the globe—often to help people whose lives had been torn apart by war. Working with war refugees solidified her opposition to all forms of war. "The person we call the enemy is Jesus disguised," she said, "and we have a duty to recognize him as such" (*National Catholic Reporter,* Oct. 20, 2000).

In 1965, Egan traveled to Rome with Dorothy Day, co-founder of the Catholic Worker movement, to persuade the bishops attending the Second Vatican Council to make a strong statement on peace issues. While Day and other Catholic peace activists fasted and prayed, Egan spoke to many of the bishops and cardinals, urging them to condemn indiscriminate warfare and to support the right to conscientious objection (the right to refuse to go to war). The Council's *Church in the Modern World* did just that.

In 1972, Egan co-founded Pax Christi USA, a national Catholic peace organization (*Pax Christi* means "peace of Christ" in Latin). As the Pax Christi representative to the United Nations, she spent years working to pass a resolution declaring conscientious objection to be a universal human right. When she finally got her wish in 1987, she called it one the greatest joys of her life.

Besides her peace work, Egan wrote extensively about Dorothy Day and Mother Teresa, both of whom were close friends. (She introduced them to each other in 1970 and wrote Mother Teresa's official biography.) Although she was not nearly as well known as those two holy women, she shared their spirituality: "My life has had a single strain," she said a few years before her death in 2000. "To see Jesus in every human being, to realize that each one is inviolable and sacred in the eyes of God, and then to translate that into everything I do. This is the heart of anything I've done" (*National Catholic Reporter,* Oct. 20, 2000).

Julie Hanlon Rubio

5

Family: The Vital Cell of Society

Introduction

As a young married couple, Bill and Teri Brandt didn't have much time for church; they were too busy working and traveling. Then Teri learned she was pregnant—with triplets. She needed to be on almost full-time bed rest for four months before the delivery.

That's when all sorts of people started visiting, often bringing Teri lunch and staying to chat. The visitors—most of whom the Brandts had never met before—were members of the Christian Family Movement (CFM), a group in which families gather to reflect on the Gospel and then act on it in their community. They had heard about the Brandts' situation and made it their mission to help the couple. When the babies arrived, the CFM families became a constant presence—they changed diapers, helped feed the babies, brought meals, and babysat so Teri could get out of the house. The CFM members helped the couple through what could have been a much more stressful time. But their outreach also profoundly affected the Brandts' lives. "It changed our minds about what Christianity and church are all about," Bill later said (*National Catholic Reporter,* Sept. 4, 1998).

It's not just families with triplets that face challenges to their well-being, as the high rate of divorce indicates. In order to address some of those challenges, the world's bishops gathered in 1980 for a synod on the family; their work was later expressed by Pope John Paul II in his 1981 apostolic exhortation *The Role of the Christian Family in the Modern World (Familiaris Consortio).*

That document highlights two truths about family life that the Brandts experienced firsthand: First, society should support families, which are its smallest and most important unit. Families give life to the next generation of society, influence the identity and character of their members, and (ideally) help each member fully realize her or his human dignity. The health and well-being of any society greatly depends on the health and well-being of its families.

Second, families are called to service. In his apostolic letter, the Pope outlines four areas in which families are called to service:

- Family members are called to serve one another in love—a type of service that is vital to the health and continuation of the family (see nos. 18–27).
- Families are called to serve life, primarily by being open to God creating new life through the married couple and by teaching children Christian and human values (see nos. 28–41).
- Families are called to serve society by helping other members of the community, especially those in need, and by working for justice (see nos. 42–48).
- As a "domestic church," families are called to participate in the life and mission of the Church (see nos. 49–64).

To some people, the call to service might seem like an added burden on families, many of whom already struggle to juggle busy schedules. But as theologian Julie Hanlon Rubio argues in *A Christian Theology of Marriage and Family*, far from being a burden, serving the wider community actually enriches and enlarges family life. The Brandts would certainly agree; after being helped by local families involved in the Christian Family Movement, they became involved in the movement themselves—along with their three young children.

Excerpt from *The Role of the Christian Family in the Modern World (Familiaris Consortio)*

by Pope John Paul II

III: Participating in the Development of Society

The Family as the First and Vital Cell of Society

42. "Since the Creator of all things has established the conjugal partnership as the beginning and basis of human society," the family is "the first and vital cell of society."

conjugal:

relating to marriage

The family has vital and organic links with society, since it is its foundation and nourishes it continually through its role of service to life: it is from the family that citizens come to birth and it is within the family that they find the first school of the social virtues that are the animating principle of the existence and development of society itself.

Thus, far from being closed in on itself, the family is by nature and vocation open to other families and to society, and undertakes its social role.

Family Life as an Experience of Communion and Sharing

43. The very experience of communion and sharing that should characterize the family's daily life represents its first and fundamental contribution to society.

The relationships between the members of the family community are inspired and guided by the law of "free giving." By respecting and fostering personal dignity in each and every one as the only basis for value, this free giving takes the form of heartfelt acceptance, encounter and dialogue, disinterested availability, generous service and deep solidarity.

Thus the fostering of authentic and mature communion between persons within the family is the first and irreplaceable school of social life, and example and stimulus for the broader community relationships marked by respect, justice, dialogue and love.

The family is thus, as the Synod Fathers recalled, the place of origin and the most effective means for humanizing and personalizing society: it makes an original contribution in depth to building up the world, by making possible a life that is properly speaking human, in particular by guarding and transmitting virtues and "values." As the Second Vatican Council states, in the family "the various generations come together and help one another to grow wiser and to harmonize personal rights with the other requirements of social living."

Synod Fathers:

A synod is a church council or gathering; here, the Pope refers to the bishops who gathered for the 1980 synod on the family.

Consequently, faced with a society that is running the risk of becoming more and more depersonalized and standardized and therefore inhuman and dehumanizing, with the negative results of many forms of escapism—such as alcoholism, drugs and even terrorism—the family possesses and continues still to release formidable energies capable of taking man out of his anonymity, keeping him conscious of his personal dignity, enriching him with deep humanity and actively placing him, in his uniqueness and unrepeatability, within the fabric of society.

The Social and Political Role

44. The social role of the family certainly cannot stop short at procreation and education, even if this constitutes its primary and irreplaceable form of expression.

Families therefore, either singly or in association, can and should devote themselves to manifold social service activities, especially in favor of the poor, or at any rate for the benefit of all people and situations that cannot be reached by the public authorities' welfare organization.

The social contribution of the family has an original character of its own, one that should be given greater recognition and more decisive encouragement, especially as the children grow up, and actually involving all its members as much as possible.

In particular, note must be taken of the ever greater importance in our society of hospitality in all its forms, from opening the door of one's home and still more of one's heart to the pleas of one's brothers and sisters, to concrete efforts to ensure that every family has its own home, as the natural environment that preserves it and makes it grow. In a special way the Christian family is called upon to listen to the Apostle's recommendation: "Practice hospitality," and therefore, imitating Christ's example and sharing in His love, to welcome the brother or sister in need: "Whoever gives to one of these little ones even a cup of cold water because he is a disciple, truly, I say to you, he shall not lose his reward" [Matt. 10:42].

The social role of families is called upon to find expression also in the form of political intervention: families should be the first to take steps to see that the laws and institutions of the State not only do not offend but support and positively defend the rights and duties of the family. Along these lines, families should grow in awareness of being "protagonists" of what is known as "family politics" and assume responsibility for transforming society; otherwise families will be the first victims of the evils that they have done no more than note with indifference. The Second Vatican Council's appeal to go beyond an individualistic ethic therefore also holds good for the family as such.

Society at the Service of the Family

45. Just as the intimate connection between the family and society demands that the family be open to and participate in society and its development, so also it requires that society should never fail in its fundamental task of respecting and fostering the family.

The family and society have complementary functions in defending and fostering the good of each and every human being. But society—more specifically the State—must recognize that "the family is a society in its own original right" and so society is under a grave obligation in its relations with the family to adhere to the principle of subsidiarity.

By virtue of this principle, the State cannot and must not take away from families the functions that they can just as well perform on their own or in free associations; instead it must positively favor and encourage as far as possible responsible initiative by families. In the conviction that the good of the family is an indispensable and essential value of the civil community, the public authorities must do everything possible to ensure that families have all those aids—economic, social, educational, political and cultural assistance—that they need in order to face all their responsibilities in a human way.

The Charter of Family Rights

46. The ideal of mutual support and development between the family and society is often very seriously in conflict with the reality of their separation and even opposition.

In fact, as was repeatedly denounced by the Synod, the situation experienced by many families in various countries is highly problematical, if not entirely negative: institutions and laws unjustly ignore the inviolable rights of the family and of the human person; and society, far from putting itself at the service of the family, attacks it violently in its values and fundamental requirements. Thus the family, which in God's plan is the basic cell of society and a subject of rights and duties before the State or any other community, finds itself the victim of society, of the delays and slowness with which it acts, and even of its blatant injustice.

usurpation:

the act of taking responsibility for something without having the right to do so

For this reason, the Church openly and strongly defends the rights of the family against the intolerable usurpations of society and the State. In particular, the Synod Fathers mentioned the following rights of the family:

- the right to exist and progress as a family, that is to say, the right of every human being, even if he or she is poor, to found a family and to have adequate means to support it;
- the right to exercise its responsibility regarding the transmission of life and to educate children; family life;
- the right to the intimacy of conjugal and family life;
- the right to the stability of the bond and of the institution of marriage;
- the right to believe in and profess one's faith and to propagate it;
- the right to bring up children in accordance with the family's own traditions and religious and cultural values, with the necessary instruments, means and institutions;

propagate:

to spread or increase

- the right, especially of the poor and the sick, to obtain physical, social, political and economic security;
- the right to housing suitable for living family life in a proper way;
- the right to expression and to representation, either directly or through associations, before the economic, social and cultural public authorities and lower authorities;
- the right to form associations with other families and institutions, in order to fulfill the family's role suitably and expeditiously;
- the right to protect minors by adequate institutions and legislation from harmful drugs, pornography, alcoholism, etc.;
- the right to wholesome recreation of a kind that also fosters family values;
- the right of the elderly to a worthy life and a worthy death;
- the right to emigrate as a family in search of a better life.

Acceding to the Synod's explicit request, the Holy See will give prompt attention to studying these suggestions in depth and to the preparation of a Charter of Rights of the Family, to be presented to the quarters and authorities concerned.

The Christian Family's Grace and Responsibility

47. The social role that belongs to every family pertains by a new and original right to the Christian family, which is based on the sacrament of marriage. By taking up the human reality of the love between husband and wife in all its implications, the sacrament gives to Christian couples and parents a power and a commitment to live their vocation as lay people and therefore to "seek the kingdom of God by engaging in temporal affairs and by ordering them according to the plan of God."

The social and political role is included in the kingly mission of service in which Christian couples share by virtue of the sacrament of marriage, and they receive both a command which they cannot ignore and a grace which sustains and stimulates them.

The Christian family is thus called upon to offer everyone a witness of generous and disinterested dedication to social matters, through a "preferential option" for the poor and disadvantaged. Therefore, advancing in its following of the Lord by special love for all the poor, it must have special concern for the hungry, the poor, the old, the sick, drug victims and those who have no family.

For a New International Order

48. In view of the worldwide dimension of various social questions nowadays, the family has seen its role with regard to the development of society extended in a completely new way: it now also involves cooperating for a new international order, since it is only in worldwide solidarity that the enormous and dramatic issues of world justice, the freedom of peoples and the peace of humanity can be dealt with and solved.

The spiritual communion between Christian families, rooted in a common faith and hope and given life by love, constitutes an inner energy that generates, spreads and develops justice, reconciliation, fraternity and peace among human beings. Insofar as it is a "small-scale Church," the Christian family is called upon, like the "large-scale Church," to be a sign of unity for the world and in this way to exercise its prophetic role by bearing witness to the Kingdom and peace of Christ, towards which the whole world is journeying.

Christian families can do this through their educational activity—that is to say by presenting to their children a model of life based on the values of truth, freedom, justice and love—both through active and responsible involvement in the authentically human growth of society and its institutions, and by supporting in various ways the associations specifically devoted to international issues.

Excerpt from *A Christian Theology of Marriage and Family*

by Julie Hanlon Rubio

During his visit to the United States in 1999, John Paul II challenged Americans to renew their commitment to their most vulnerable citizens and neighbors. He asked them, as he asked them many times before, to choose life, which "involves rejecting every form of violence: the violence of poverty and hunger, which oppresses so many human beings; the violence of armed conflict, which does not resolve but only increases divisions and tensions"; as well as violence against the unborn.[1] In his speeches, the pope drew upon a long and rich tradition of Catholic social teaching that emphasizes solidarity and the common good.[2] This body of teaching sees human persons as essentially social beings who are unable to be fully human alone.

Recall that John Paul II sees the mythical story of Adam and Eve in the book of Genesis as a story about the necessity of human relationship. He emphasizes that Adam looks at all the creatures God had created up until that point and finds them unsuitable mates. Only when God puts Adam to sleep and creates Eve from his rib does Adam, overcome with joy, exclaim, "This at last is bone of my bones and flesh of my flesh" (Gen 2:23). This is the first biblical story Christians read, and in it they come to know that they are called to mutual and self-giving relationships.

What begins with Adam and Eve in the most intense fashion gets extended by analogy to all human beings. Human beings are not meant to live alone. Rather, they are called to live in relationship—in community—with one another. Thus they are bound to look beyond their own personal good in order to seek the good of the larger community of persons to which they belong. In the words of the pope, human beings have the duty to "situate particular interests within a coherent vision of the common good."[3] This means that individuals, and even individual families, cannot just take care of their own. Catholic social teaching requires them to value the good of others as well. Furthermore,

Christians have a responsibility to practice the value of solidarity, which resembles the common good in that it refers to a commitment beyond oneself and one's family, but differs in that it calls for a specific obligation to serve and empower the poor. Valuing solidarity inevitably leads to embracing the struggle for justice with and on behalf of the poor and marginalized.[4]

Catholic social teaching centering on these themes addresses primarily individuals, not families. However, the tradition holds that the family is a domestic church with both a personal and a social vocation. Families, as small church communities, foster loving relationships, teach about the faith, ritualize important occasions, and serve the needs of the larger church and the world. "Domestic church" language does not simply suggest a similarity between families and churches; it insists that families are small churches with a responsibility for fostering love within and living Christian social values outside its boundaries. Families are communities of love with a social mission. John Paul II has made this point more strongly than any recent pope, saying that the family is "called to offer everyone a witness of generous and disinterested dedication to social matters through a 'preferential option' for the poor and disadvantaged."[5]

This social mandate of the family stands as perhaps the greatest strength of Catholic social teaching on the family. In contrast to those who argue that being a good family is primarily a private task, Catholic teaching emphasizes that moral thinking about the family makes sense only when done in a communal context.

The idea that families should incorporate the values of solidarity and the common good into their lives is complemented by other aspects of Catholic teaching on the family. For instance, . . . recent reforms in the Catholic wedding liturgy signal a renewed attention to ways a couple's relationship exists in the context of the larger community. The church asks couples who seek marriage to make the participation of those who gather for the wedding ceremony a priority in order to underscore the idea that all who attend the wedding witness to it and are involved in the sealing of the couple's bond. No longer can couples view their marriage as simply a union of two. In the new wedding ceremony, as a couple opens itself to the community, the community promises to support the couple in good times and bad. The new liturgy guidelines suggest that marriage, a relationship that opens itself to all, must entail a commitment to the good of others.

Similarly, . . . when Pope John Paul II speaks directly to the family as opposed to married couples, he asserts that families have four tasks: loving each other, serving life, serving the church, and taking appropriate social-political action on behalf of vulnerable people in their society. Clearly, family members are called to do more than simply love each other; their work begins but does not end there. According to the best of the Catholic tradition, the family cannot concern itself solely with the welfare of its own members; it has an obligation to take seriously the welfare of local, national, and even international communities. The family is, for John Paul II, a communion of disciples of Christ that must situate its own good in the context of the common good and make a commitment to serve the poor in some way.

Catholic social teaching provides a helpful starting point for thinking through the relationship between family and society, for it calls Christian families to uphold values of solidarity and the common good as they make the most crucial moral decisions of their lives: decisions about work, time, and money.

Work

What role should work play in contemporary families? Most historians of the family agree that families in the postindustrial world differ in fundamental ways from families in earlier times because they do not normally find their group identity in their work.[6] Because most families do not run farms or shops together, the work they do no longer defines them. Rather, families stand apart from the jobs individual parents do to support them. No longer centered around a common mission, the family's function is uncertain. In the age of the welfare state, when many families receive from the government services they cannot provide for themselves (like elder care, food stamps, and health care), the function of the family grows more questionable. In recent decades, when more and more middle-class families have begun buying services they used to perform (like meal preparation, house cleaning, and day care), family goals have become even more uncertain. Thus today it is necessary to ask, "What does the family do? What would it mean for the family to be itself, as John Paul II asks it to be?"[7]

Many would argue that the contemporary family exists primarily to nurture and support its members. This view assumes a romantic ideal of the family and asserts the necessity of a commitment to care for family members above all else. . . .

The work vs. family dilemma is not simply a question of individualism vs. self-sacrifice for a greater good. In reality, many goods are at stake when parents make decisions about work: the benefits of parents' spending time with their children, the benefits of children's exposure to different adult role models, the gifts parents have to offer to communities. Questions regarding the ethics of work, when viewed in the larger context of solidarity and the common good, become more difficult, but more properly situated for a Christian discussion of what the family is about.

Time

Questions about work are intimately related to questions about time, for most families feel that they lack the time to be the kind of families they want to be. Even if families commit to work for the common good, they also need time for themselves. An often-cited 1989 survey of American families reported that most Americans see lack of time as the crucial problem facing families today.[8] Lack of family time affects not only parents who work more and consequently see their children less. Children today also see their grandparents, aunts, and uncles less because of increased mobility. Parents see their teenage sons and daughters less because more of them work part-time. Husbands and wives find it harder to take time for each other. Most agree that more time would help them and others to be better families. Anyone who has experienced the pressures of contemporary family life would doubtless agree. Time poses a serious problem for many families. If society values families, it certainly should make it possible for families to spend more time together.

Some changes are already occurring. The government has finally made twelve weeks of unpaid family leave a given for large businesses, and more employers offer flextime, job sharing, or reduced hours for reduced pay. Many people are forced to work part-time; others choose to work part-time or downsize into less demanding jobs because they want more time with those they love most.

What, then, can be done with this time? Why do families want time? There is a danger that more family time will simply encourage greater privatization in American culture. If families simply spend more time together at the mall or in front of the TV set, they will have gained little. Yet many families may find it hard to think of time any differently. As sociologist Robert Bellah notes, Americans have developed a very private ideal of leisure. Especially since the rise of the middle class after World War II, private leisure came to be seen as the most important element of the good life, for "here intimacy, solidarity, and voluntary accomplishments in sport, art, or craft flourished, crowned life, and made it whole."[9] The family gathered around the TV set or the backyard barbecue became the symbol of success.

Catholic social teaching calls this idealization of private leisure into question and asks families to think not only of their own interests, but also the interests of those in their communities most in need of help. To be valuable, the time families spend together need not be private. In fact, Bellah claims that most people derive little satisfaction from the most typical of leisure activities, TV-watching. He argues that when we engage in leisure that is "mildly demanding but inherently meaningful— reading a good book, repairing the car, talking to someone we love, or even cooking the family meal—we are more apt to find that we are 'relaxed.'"[10] Would not leisure spent in activities that help others have a similar effect?

Significantly, Catholic social teaching calls families to spend some time serving the common good and practicing solidarity. Families might serve the common good in a variety of ways, including volunteering at the school their children attend, participating in civic or religious organizations, and becoming active in their own neighborhood. All of this contributes to the common good. However, if middle-class families serve only other middle-class families, then the common good is only partly realized and solidarity with the poor and marginalized remains a distant ideal.

The Parenting for Peace and Justice Network, based in St. Louis, gives an example of an alternative model. Families who belong to the network engage in service activities together, share ideas about how to live more simply, and believe it is possible to parent well without abandoning a strong commitment to those in need.[11] The growing Voluntary Simplicity movement, which involves people all over the country who attempt to live on less money, scale back work commitments, and spend time doing what they really want to do, also emphasizes community service.[12]

Families can use more time to build their own small community of disciples by serving the common good. Each family must decide on its own specific mission. What is important is that they use the time they gain not to isolate themselves from society but to gain the freedom and space they need to think about what they can do together for others.

Money

How do commitments to solidarity and the common good affect families' choices about how to spend money? Is this an important ethical question? Some might argue that spending is a private issue because each family is different and spends relatively little in comparison to businesses or governments. Contemporary culture tends to trivialize this aspect of the moral life, ignoring the reality that the way families choose to spend their money significantly affects their lives and the lives of others. However, if one takes Catholic social teaching seriously, financial decisions have ethical import.

In contrast, a 1995 story from the Business Section of the *Los Angeles Times* provides readers with a map showing how an average college-educated couple can buy a house, send their kids to college, and live comfortably while saving enough to become millionaires by the time they retire.[13] It suggests that most families can get out of debt and achieve the same goal by following the prudent example of this ideal couple. What is presented as a simple article on personal finances is in fact a statement of important values. This couple has one major goal in life: wealth. They succeed because, after more than forty years of frugality, they end up as millionaires who can spend their time traveling around the world. To achieve their goal, the couple relies upon two steady, uninterrupted incomes. The map does not allow for exploring different career options, volunteering, or easing workloads when children arrive. It does not consider the social import of the couple's work or the fact that they will miss out on time alone, time with children, and time spent in nonlucrative community activities. The money the couple earns goes directly into necessary expenditures and long-term investments. . . .

Endnotes

1. John Paul II, "Speech at Arrival," St. Louis, January 26, 1999, *www.vatican.va/holy_father/john_paul_ii/travels/*.

2. This tradition of writings from the popes and bishops on social issues like war and peace, work and workers, and race and poverty is usually traced to 1891, when Pope Leo XIII wrote on the labor question and asserted that workers have certain inalienable rights, including the right to unionize. Ever since then, most of the church's popes and many of its national conferences of bishops have addressed the important social issues of their day.

3. John Paul II, *On Social Concern* (Washington, DC: United States Catholic Conference, 1987), 38.

4. See Donal Dorr, *Option for the Poor: A Hundred Years of Catholic Social Teaching,* rev. ed. (Maryknoll, NY: Orbis, 1992), 2.

5. John Paul II, *On the Family* (Washington, DC: United States Catholic Conference, 1981), no. 47.

6. See Judith Stacey, *Brave New Families: Stories of Domestic Upheaval in Late Twentieth Century America* (New York: Basic Books, 1991), 3–19.

7. *On the Family,* no. 17.

8. Mark Mellman et al., "Family Time, Family Values," in *Rebuilding the Nest,* 73–92.

9. Robert Bellah et al., *The Good Society* (New York: Vintage 1991), 23.

10. Ibid., 255.

11. James and Kathleen McGinnis, *Parenting for Peace and Justice: Ten Years Later* (Maryknoll, NY: Orbis, 1990).

12. See Duane Elgin, *Voluntary Simplicity: Toward a Way of Life That Is Outwardly Simple, Inwardly Rich,* rev. ed. (New York: Quill, 1993).

13. Daniel Gaines, "Mapping Out Your Own Road," *Los Angeles Times,* October 1, 1995, D2.

For Reflection

1. Why is it important for families to spend time together serving the common good and practicing solidarity? Summarize the reasons given in these readings.
2. Choose five of the rights of families listed by the pope in *The Role of Christian Families in the Modern World,* number 46. Give your community a letter grade for each right, depending on how well it upholds them. Explain the reason for each grade, and offer some suggestions for how your community could do better.
3. How does your own family serve others? What would need to happen in order for your family to do more to serve the common good and practice solidarity with the poor?

Profile

The Christian Family Movement

Reaching out to help others—like Bill and Teri Brandt, the couple expecting triplets (see the introduction to this chapter)—is part of what members of the Christian Family Movement do. But CFM is much more than another service organization.

The origins of the group date to 1943 when a handful of Chicago men began meeting on a regular basis with a local priest. They were among the many groups inspired by Catholic Action, an international movement in which ordinary Catholics applied their faith to social problems. Catholic Action proposed a three-step process for such work, summarized as "see, judge, act." Participants first gathered facts about the problem ("see"), then analyzed the problem in light of the Gospel ("judge"), and finally took action to address the problem ("act").

The Chicago men's group used this process to reflect on the marriage relationship. Eventually, some of their wives began forming similar groups, and by the late 1940s, many men's and women's groups had merged. In 1949, Catholic Action groups for married couples from around the country gathered for a national conference, and the Christian Family Movement was born.

Today, the Christian Family Movement consists of networks of families that meet regularly to reflect on the Gospel and Catholic social teaching—and then put their insights into action, whether that means reaching out to a grieving family or bringing food and blankets to a local homeless shelter. By helping families extend their circle of love into the community, the Christian Family Movement realizes one of the central themes of Catholic social teaching. Says Sue Szymczak, a member of the Christian Family Movement group that helped the Brandts: "You could kind of call us one big extended family" (*National Catholic Reporter,* Sept. 4, 1998).

Cesar Chavez

6

Human Work

Introduction

As a top-level manager at the multibillion dollar fruit and vegetable company Chiquita Brands, Bob Ehrsam knew his employer had a few bad habits—breaking up farm workers' unions, bribing foreign government officials, and contracting with companies that pollute the environment, to name a few. Ehrsam strongly objected to those practices, but what could he do? Many people would be tempted to ignore the situation rather than rock the boat; others would just quit.

But choosing either of those options would not have changed anything at Chiquita. So instead, Ehrsam challenged the company to quit its bad habits, arguing that socially responsible business practices could actually benefit the company. And as Dennis O'Connor recounts in his article "By Their Fruits You Shall Know Them," the efforts of Ehrsam and others were not in vain. Today, Chiquita Brands is publicly committed to socially responsible business practices.

Ehrsam was inspired to take action after reading *Economic Justice for All*, the United States Conference of Catholic Bishops' 1986 pastoral letter that analyzed the U.S. economy in light of Catholic social teaching. The bishops spent years crafting the pastoral letter with the input of experts and ordinary people; when it was released, it generated much discussion and a certain amount of controversy. Some people thought the Church shouldn't speak on economics or labor issues, but those have been central themes of Catholic social teaching since Pope Leo XIII issued the first modern social encyclical in 1891, *On Capital and Labor (Rerum Novarum)*. The Church teaches about work because when work fulfills its basic purposes, it becomes an important way for people to relate to God.

Pope John Paul II outlined three basic purposes of work in his 1981 encyclical *On Human Work (Laborem Exercens)*:

- First, work is meant to express human dignity. Human creativity—the ability to imagine something new, and then make it real—is one of the ways in which people are made in the image of God. When people create something through work (even something as simple as a clean floor), they reflect the activity of the Creator of the universe (see *On Human Work,* nos. 4 and 9). Even when work is hard, the person who does it for the sake of something good collaborates in a certain way with the redemptive work of Jesus Christ (see no. 27).
- Second, work is meant to enable people to get what they need to support themselves and their family in dignity (see no. 10).
- And finally, work is meant to contribute to the common good—that is, the good of all (see no. 10).

The extent to which work fulfills its threefold purpose is the measure of its justice. The bottom line is that work should always be directed toward the good of the human person; it should treat workers as human beings, not machines whose only purpose is production.

In the years since *Economic Justice for All* was released, an increasing number of U.S. Catholics have followed Bob Ehrsam's example by examining the moral and social dimension of their work. That's an especially important responsibility for workers in the United States; as the driving force behind the world's largest economy, their decisions have consequences far beyond their own careers. As you read the following selections, consider the implications for your own work.

Excerpts from *Economic Justice for All: Pastoral Letter on Catholic Social Teaching and the U.S. Economy*

by the United States Conference of Catholic Bishops

C. Working for Greater Justice: Persons and Institutions

96. The economy of this nation has been built by the labor of human hands and minds. Its future will be forged by the ways persons direct all this work toward greater justice. The economy is not a machine that operates according to its own inexorable laws, and persons are not mere objects tossed about by economic forces. Pope John Paul II has stated that "human

inexorable:

unstoppable or unchangeable

work is a key, probably the essential key, to the whole social question."[1] The Pope's understanding of work includes virtually all forms of productive human activity: agriculture, entrepreneurship, industry, the care of children, the sustaining of family life, politics, medical care, and scientific research. Leisure, prayer, celebration, and the arts are also central to the realization of human dignity and to the development of a rich cultural life. It is in their daily work, however, that persons become the subjects and creators of the economic life of the nation.[2] Thus, it is primarily through their daily labor that people make their most important contributions to economic justice.

97. All work has a threefold moral significance. First, it is a principal way that people exercise the distinctive human capacity for self-expression and self-realization. Second, it is the ordinary way for human beings to fulfill their material needs. Finally, work enables people to contribute to the well-being of the larger community. Work is not only for one's self. It is for one's family, for the nation, and indeed for the benefit of the entire human family.[3]

98. These three moral concerns should be visible in the work of all, no matter what their role in the economy: blue collar workers, managers, homemakers, politicians, and others. They should also govern the activities of the many different, overlapping communities and institutions that make up society: families, neighborhoods, small businesses, giant corporations, trade unions, the various levels of government, international organizations, and a host of other human associations including communities of faith.

99. Catholic social teaching calls for respect for the full richness of social life. The need for vital contributions from different human associations—ranging in size from the family to government—has been classically expressed in Catholic social teaching in the "principle of subsidiarity":

> "Just as it is gravely wrong to take from individuals what they can accomplish by their own initiative and industry and give it to the community, so also it is an injustice and at the same time a grave evil and disturbance of right order to assign a greater and higher association what lesser and subordinate organizations can do. For every social activity ought of its very nature to furnish help *(subsidium)* to the members of the body social, and never destroy and absorb them."[4]

100. This principle guarantees institutional pluralism. It provides space for freedom, initiative, and creativity on the part of many social agents. At the same time, it insists that *all* these agents should work in ways that help build up the social body. Therefore, in all their activities these groups should be working in ways that express their distinctive capacities for action, that help meet human needs, and that make true contributions to the common good of the human community. The task of creating a more just U.S. economy is a vocation of all and depends on strengthening the virtues of public service and responsible citizenship in personal life and on all levels of institutional life.[5]

101. Without attempting to describe the tasks of all the different groups that make up society, we want to point to the specific rights and duties of some of the persons and institutions whose work for justice will be

particularly important to the future of the U.S. economy. These rights and duties are among the concrete implications of the principle of subsidiarity. Further implications will be discussed in Chapter IV of this letter.

1. Working People and Labor Unions

102. Though John Paul II's understanding of work is a very inclusive one, it fully applies to those customarily called "workers" or "labor" in the United States. Labor has great dignity, so great that all who are able to work are obligated to do so. The duty to work derives both from God's command and from a responsibility to one's own humanity and to the common good.[6] The virtue of industriousness is also an expression of a person's dignity and solidarity with others. All working people are called to contribute to the common good by seeking excellence in production and service.

103. Because work is this important, people have a right to employment. In return for their labor, workers have a right to wages and other benefits sufficient to sustain life in dignity. As Pope Leo XIII stated, every working person has "the right of securing things to sustain life."[7] The way power is distributed in a free market economy frequently gives employers greater bargaining power than employees in the negotiation of labor contracts. Such unequal power may press workers into a choice between an inadequate wage or no wage at all. But justice, not charity, demands certain minimum wage guarantees. The provision of wages and other benefits sufficient to support a family in dignity

free market economy:

an unregulated economic system in which goods and services are exchanged at a rate determined only by their supply and the demand for them

is a basic necessity to prevent this exploitation of workers. The dignity of workers also requires adequate health care, security for old age or disability, unemployment compensation, healthful working conditions, weekly rest, periodic holidays for recreation and leisure, and reasonable security against arbitrary dismissal.[8] These provisions are all essential if workers are to be treated as persons rather than simply a "factor of production."

104. The Church fully supports the right of workers to form unions or other associations to secure their rights to fair wages and working conditions. This is a specific application of the more general right to associate. In the words of Pope John Paul II, "The experience of history teaches that organizations of this type are an indispensable element of social life, especially in modern industrial societies."[9] Unions may also legitimately resort to strikes where this is the only available means to the justice owed to workers.[10] No one may deny the right to organize without attacking human dignity itself. Therefore, we firmly oppose organized efforts, such as those regrettably now seen in this country, to break existing unions and prevent workers from organizing. Migrant agricultural workers today are particularly in need of the protection, including the right to organize and bargain collectively. U.S. labor law reform is needed to meet these problems as well as to provide more timely and effective remedies for unfair labor practices.

105. Denial of the right to organize has been pursued ruthlessly in many countries beyond our borders. We vehemently oppose violations of the freedom to associate, wherever they occur, for they are an intolerable attack on social solidarity.

106. Along with the rights of workers and unions go a number of important responsibilities. Individual workers have obligations to their employers, and trade unions also have duties to society as a whole. Union management in particular carries a strong responsibility for the good name of the entire union movement. Workers must use their collective power to contribute to the well-being of the whole community and should avoid pressing demands whose fulfillment would damage the common

collectivism:

a philosophy that emphasizes the importance of the group (collective) over the individual

good and the rights of more vulnerable members of society.[11] It should be noted, however, that wages paid to workers are but one of the factors affecting the competitiveness of industries. Thus, it is unfair to expect unions to make concessions if managers and shareholders do not make at least equal sacrifices. . . .

2. Owners and Managers

110. The economy's success in fulfilling the demands of justice will depend on how its vast resources and wealth are managed. Property owners, managers, and investors of financial capital must all contribute to creating a more just society. Securing economic justice depends heavily on the leadership of men and women in business and on the wise investment by private enterprises. Pope John Paul II has pointed out, "The degree of well-being which society today enjoys would be unthinkable without the dynamic figure of the business person, whose function consists of organizing human labor and the means of production so as to give rise to the goods and services necessary for the prosperity and progress of the community."[12] The freedom of entrepreneurship, business, and finance should be protected, but the accountability of this freedom to the common good and the norms of justice must be assured.

111. Persons in management face many hard choices each day, choices on which the well-being of many others depends. Commitment to the public good and not simply the private good of their firms is at the heart of what it means to call their work a vocation and not simply a career or a job. We believe that the norms and priorities discussed in this letter can be of help as they pursue their important tasks. The duties of individuals in the business world, however, do not exhaust the ethical dimensions of business and finance. The size of a firm or bank is in many cases an indicator of relative power. Large corporations and large financial institutions have considerable power to help shape economic institutions within the United States and throughout the world. With this power goes responsibility and the need for those who manage it to be held to moral and institutional accountability.

112. Business and finance have the duty to be faithful trustees of the resources at their disposal. No one can ever own capital resources absolutely or control their use without regard for others and society as a whole.[13] This applies first of all to land and natural resources. Short-term profits reaped at the cost of depletion of natural resources or the pollution of the environment violate this trust.

113. Resources created by human industry are also held in trust. Owners and managers have not created this capital on their own. They have

benefited from the work of many others and from the local communities that support their endeavors.[14] They are accountable to these workers and communities when making decisions. For example, reinvestment in technological innovation is often considered crucial for the long-term viability of a firm. The use of financial resources solely in pursuit of short-term profits can stunt the production of needed goods and services; a broader vision of managerial responsibility is needed.

114. The Catholic tradition has long defended the right to private ownership of productive property.[15] This right is an important element in a just economic policy. It enlarges our capacity for creativity and initiative.[16] Small and medium-sized farms, businesses, and entrepreneurial enterprises are among the most creative and efficient sectors of our economy. They should be highly valued by the people of the United States, as are land ownership and home ownership. Widespread distribution of property can help avoid excessive concentration of economic and political power. For these reasons ownership should be made possible for a broad sector of our population.[17]

115. The common good may sometimes demand that the right to own be limited by public involvement in the planning or ownership of certain sectors of the economy. Support of private ownership does not mean that anyone has the right to unlimited accumulation of wealth. "Private property does not constitute for anyone an absolute or unconditional right. No one is justified in keeping for his exclusive use what he does not need, when others lack necessities."[18] Pope John Paul II has referred to limits placed on ownership by the duty to serve the common good as a "social mortgage" on private property.[19] For example, these limits are the basis of society's exercise of eminent domain over privately owned land needed for roads or other essential public goods.

statism:

a system in which the state, or government, plans the economy

The Church's teaching opposes collectivist and statist economic approaches. But it also rejects the notion that a free market automatically produces justice. Therefore, as Pope John Paul II has argued, "One cannot exclude the socialization, in suitable conditions, of certain means of production."[20] The determination of when such conditions exist must be made on a case by case basis in light of the demands of the common good.

116. United States business and financial enterprises can also help determine the justice or injustice of the world economy. They are not all-powerful, but their real power is unquestionable. Transnational corporations and financial institutions

socialization:

In this context, socialization is the process by which the government takes over private industries.

can make positive contributions to development and global solidarity. Pope John Paul II has pointed out, however, that the desire to maximize profits and reduce cost of natural resources and labor has often tempted these transnational enterprises to behavior that increases inequality and decreases the stability of the international order.[21] By collaborating with those national governments that serve their citizens justly and with intergovernmental agencies, these corporations can contribute to overcoming the desperate plight of many persons throughout the world. . . .

Endnotes

1. *On Human Work*, 3.

2. Ibid., 5, 6.

3. Ibid., 6, 10.

4. *Quadragesimo Anno*, 79. The meaning of this principle is not always accurately understood. For studies of its interpretation in Catholic teaching see: Calvez and Perrin in John F. Cronin, *Catholic Social Principles*, (Milwaukee: Bruce, 1950), 328-342; Johannes Messner, "Freedom as a Principle of Social Order: An Essay in the Substance of Subsidiary Function," *Modern Schoolman* 28 (1951): 97–110; Richard E. Mulcahy, "Subsidiarity," *New Catholic Encyclopedia* vol. 13 (New York: McGraw-Hill, 1966), 762; Franz H. Mueller, "The Principle of Subsidiarity in Christian Tradition," *American Catholic Sociological Review* 4 (October 1943): 144–157; Oswald von Nell-Breuning, "Zur Sozialreform, Erwagungen zum Subisdi aritatsprinzip," *Stimmen der Zeit* 157, Bd. 81 (1955–1956): 1–11; id., "Subsidiarity," *Sacramentum Mundi*, vol. 6 (New York: Herder and Herder, 1970), 6, 114–116; Arthur Fridolin Utz, *Formen und Grenzen des Subsidiaritatsprinzips* (Heidelberg: F. H. Kerle Verlag, 1956); id., "The Princple of Subsidiarity and Contemporary Natural

Law," *Natural Law Forum* 3 (1958): 170–183; id., *Grundsatze der Sozialpolitik: Solidaritat und Subsidiaritat in der Alterversicherung* (Stuttgart: Sewald Verlag, 1969).

5. *Pastoral Constitution*, 31.

6. *On Human Work*, 16.

7. *Rerum Novarum*, 62; see also 9.

8. *On Human Work*, 19.

9. Ibid., 20.

10. Ibid.

11. Ibid.

12. Pope John Paul II, Address to Business Men and Economic Managers (Milan, May 22, 1983) in *L'Osservatore Romano*, weekly edition in English (June 20, 1983): 9:1.

13. Thomas Aquinas, *Summa Theologiae*, IIa, IIae, q. 66.

14. As Pope John Paul II has stated: This gigantic and powerful instrument—the whole collection of the means of production that in a sense are considered synonymous with 'capital'—is the result of work and bears the signs of human labor," *On Human Work*, 12.

15. *Rerum Novarum*, 10, 15, 36.

16. *Mater et Magistra*, 109.

17. *Rerum Novarum*, 65, 66; *Mater et Magistra*, 115.

18. *On the Development of Peoples*, 23.

19. Pope John Paul II, Opening Address at the Puebla Conference (Puebla, Mexico, January 28, 1979), in John Eagleson and Phillip Schaerper, eds., *Puebla and Beyond*, 67.

20. *On Human Work*, 14.

21. Ibid., 17.

Excerpts from "By Their Fruits You Shall Know Them: Can Catholics Make a Difference for Justice in the Business World?"

by Dennis O'Connor

In the dining room of a Guatemala City guest house, a group of Americans is clustered around a big map of Guatemala. They are watching an animated representative from the union syndicate Unsitragua jabbing his right forefinger at points along the country's Pacific coast.

"There, there, and all along here," he says, North American multinational companies, including Cincinnati-based Chiquita Brands, are operating banana plantations that their corporate officials claim are independently run small enterprises. The union rep complains that Unsitragua is not allowed near these plantations, but if they are run by multinational companies, the union has the right to try to organize the workers.

While the visitors from the United States—a delegation of teachers, businesspeople, and church employees from the Archdiocese of Cincinnati—sip tea, the union coordinator studies each of their faces. Speaking through a translator, he tells the group that if companies are engaged in these kinds of operations, they are bypassing Guatemalan laws limiting foreign companies' ownership of farms by setting up local "fronts" for the corporation.

"I hope you will tell the people of Cincinnati that this is going on down here," the representative says. "Ask Chiquita if they are doing this. They will listen to you."

Michael Gable, director of the Archdiocese of Cincinnati's Missions Office, nods thanks to the man and then explains to the delegation the history of the longstanding economic relationship between Cincinnati and Central America. Coffee beans and bananas grown in Honduras, Guatemala, Nicaragua, Costa Rica, Panama, and parts of Mexico have helped to fuel the engines of such venerated icons of American capitalism as consumer-goods giant Procter & Gamble, fruit company Chiquita

Brands International, and the nation's largest grocer, the Kroger Company—all based in Cincinnati.

Gradually it dawns on the group that much of the stable and diverse economy that has provided relatively high-paying jobs and other benefits to the people of the greater Cincinnati region has been built on the backs of Central American and other Third World workers.

The delegation had made its way to Guatemala City as part of the Archdiocese of Cincinnati's initiative "Global Solidarity: Focus Central America." Launched in 1998, the five-year program was directed by a group that included a former Chiquita executive, local social activists, instructors at Cincinnati's Xavier University, and staff of the archdiocese's mission and social-action offices.

The initiative has provided an intriguing experiment in involving Catholic business leaders in examining how principles of Catholic social teaching might be applied in practical ways by multinational corporations.

Two of its aims have been to create awareness among consumers about the plight of Central American workers and to promote greater ethical sensitivity at Chiquita, Procter & Gamble, and Kroger. Church leaders have talked with company bosses about workers' rights. Procter & Gamble, which produces Folgers and Millstone coffees, has been urged to purchase fair-trade coffee. The dialogue has also explored how globalization has forced workers from the same Central American countries where these companies have banana and coffee plantations to emigrate to Cincinnati.

The members of the Guatemala delegation as well as others involved in the initiative were brought to ponder their place in this economic universe: What responsibilities do Catholic business executives have to seek the greater good, even when it may be in conflict with achieving financial goals or other corporate objectives? What can individuals do to effect change, to make sure that their own companies are doing what they can to provide for the poor?

Do Catholics have an obligation within their secular vocations to place the church's call for social justice in front of other demands? In a difficult economic environment, how should a company deal with issues such as just wages and workforce reductions? Do Catholic businesspeople actually embrace the tenets of Catholic social teaching and act upon them, or do they either ignore or pay lip service to them and carry on with business as usual? . . .

Applied Social Teaching

"If business managers really use Catholic social teaching as a principle for their daily work lives, then they will understand that everything boils down to the dignity of the human being in all corners," says Bob Ehrsam, a former Chiquita manager and a leader in the Archdiocese of Cincinnati's Global Solidarity initiative. "That is especially true in . . . the challenges of globalization. It's trickier out there now. There are moral minefields everywhere for someone claiming to have a Christian perspective on running a business."

Part of the message of Catholic social teaching has been a call to recognize that the needs of the poor take priority over the desires of the rich; the rights of workers over the maximization of profits; and the preservation of the environment over uncontrolled industrial expansion. The bishops have challenged Catholics in the United States to make a fundamental "option for the poor" in the marketplace.

But within the context of the global economy, opting for the poor, promoting human dignity, and pursuing the common good often appear at odds with a business culture that "demands efficiency and profitability at nearly any cost," says Ehrsam.

Ehrsam says he experienced this firsthand in confrontations with his former bosses at Chiquita. He had closely read the U.S. Catholic bishops' 1986 pastoral letter on the economy called "Economic Justice for All" and looked for ways to apply some of its message to his own decisions.

"I had to pick and choose where I made my stand," he says. In charge of several areas of purchasing, he worked to eliminate the time-honored tradition of bribing corrupt government officials. And he refused to award contracts to agricultural companies in Honduras that were known to be polluting the environment.

"It was easy to speak up, but sometimes I know I sounded countercultural within the company. I was asking questions about issues such as safety and the environment and whether we were doing the moral thing. But ultimately we helped set many of these issues straight," even if ethical solutions were first dismissed as too costly. "I think that Chiquita came to realize that, at least in a lot of cases, decisions that were framed in good, moral, Catholic social thinking also turned out to be good business decisions."

Ehrsam particularly questioned the company's strategy of union-busting in Central America.

"For years I had urged the owners of the company to sit down and rethink the time and energy they spent trying to dismantle their organized labor structure," he recalls. "It seemed like a foolish business strategy to me. I wasn't just concerned about the bottom line, but I also knew that these unions were critical in helping workers attain the rights they had already gained, such as certain wage rates and living standards.

"Ultimately I showed my bosses that the amount of time and resources they spent in union-busting was more than they would have to give up in any concessions made to the unions. It was an eye-opener for the owners." And it was also a way for Ehrsam to put into practice in his own workplace the lessons he had learned from Catholic social teaching. . . .

Love and Layoffs

Several Catholic-led initiatives today attempt to counter that sense of moral isolation within the halls of business. Some of them are academically sponsored programs such as the Arrupe Program in Social Ethics for Business at the Woodstock Theological Center at Georgetown University. In the program, corporate chiefs spend days or weeks examining issues such as the ethical considerations in corporate takeovers or how to create an ethical corporate climate. Participants at Woodstock-sponsored gatherings have come from such places as the Brookings Institute, Chase Manhattan Bank, FMC Corporation, and the World Bank.

But even more interesting is Woodstock's nationwide business conference, comprised of 19 chapters of business leaders in Washington, Milwaukee, and New York City, among other urban centers, which addresses the practical day-to-day issues confronting business leaders against the backdrop of scripture readings and with topical background articles. Terry Armstrong, director of the Woodstock Business Conference, says participants discuss these topics in a way that promotes greater understanding, sound decision-making, and action grounded in moral values.

Conference members are invited to participate in a process modeled after the Jesuits' 30-day Ignatian retreat, Armstrong notes. It takes up to a couple of years to fully examine an issue such as moral decision-making, lay vocations in the marketplace, or pursuing values in business.

Lofty ideals, certainly. But the objective is to put the lessons learned from these discussions to work.

Exploring those lessons was what energized Gregory F. Augustine Pierce, owner of ACTA Publications and an active member of BEEJ—which constitutes the Chicago unit of the Woodstock Business Conference.

"There are no simple answers, especially in this discussion" about being a responsible business manager, Pierce says. "So we are not trying to come up with simple answers. Our group of business leaders is seeking to find some wisdom in each other's experience and then apply that as best we can in our own companies."

In the years since the group's founding, business leaders who have been involved in the Chicago dialogue have examined issues such as how a company might deal with layoffs, the need for stewardship in business, just wages, and the ethical formation of the business executive.

"We sit down and tackle very tough issues," Pierce says. "There isn't any 'What would Jesus do?' in this. We will really dig into an issue for a couple years, looking at it inside and out, and we frame it in an ethical context. We ask, 'How do we get the courage to do what needs to be done [and] to do the right thing?' And then we ask, 'How does the church help us do all that?'

"This group gives people what they can't get anywhere else," Pierce says. "You don't have these kinds of discussions in the secular arena. This is a unique perspective where Jesus is the Way, the Truth, and the Light. And we see if there is a way that you can run a business successfully in a capitalist economy and still be true to your religious faith. After 15 years, we are still at it."

One of the first studies the Chicago group tackled was dealing with layoffs.

"The members of our group are by and large small business owners, so the worry about laying somebody off is a real issue, a real person, not some number," he says. "It was a real issue of 'How do you really love somebody, then lay them off?' We had members of our group who faced that very question when it was a family member who had to be let go. It becomes an issue of studying the results of your decision. In this case, what if you don't lay them off? Does your company survive or do you go under? And if you don't survive, what are the results of that? Many more people are affected by your decision to save one job. Tough calls, very tough decisions."

The primary benefit of the Chicago project is the mutual support the business leaders offer each other. And that mutual support is critical for successful application of Catholic social thought in the long haul, says Notre Dame's Williams.

Taking a Stand

But sometimes businesspeople find themselves in situations that require actions where support may not immediately be available. That was the case for Julia Wagner, a research and development employee at Procter & Gamble.

In late 2002 Wagner learned by way of a company e-mail that P&G was releasing its first-ever policy governing how the consumer goods giant could conduct stem-cell research—studies that scientists believe show great promise in fighting diseases such as Parkinson's, diabetes, and Alzheimer's.

"The policy left the door open, just a tiny crack, for the company to conduct embryonic stem-cell research," she says. According to the policy, P&G would attempt other forms of stem-cell research first, such as adult stem-cell studies and research on animal materials, but it clearly defined P&G's steps toward embryonic studies.

"From the beginning, when the policy was issued, I started a lot of conversations with fellow workers within the halls of Procter & Gamble because I was uncomfortable with the policy. It was in direct conflict with my faith."

Wagner contacted leadership at her parish, and she ultimately asked the Archdiocese of Cincinnati to weigh in on the company's policy. She e-mailed employees she knew were Catholic and posted information on a company bulletin board that corporate chiefs monitored, asking them for comments and why such a policy was deemed necessary. Meanwhile, Archbishop Daniel E. Pilarczyk issued a statement questioning P&G's policy, noting that if embryonic stem-cell research was on the horizon for the firm, it was in the wrong.

Scott Syfert, an engineer for Procter & Gamble, also spoke out, noting that "Procter is a great company . . . but in this particular case, they made a mistake."

A company spokeswoman said that Procter currently was not conducting any studies using embryonic stem cells, but they reserved the right to do so. Wagner says she maintains her vigil on the matter, noting that she sometimes worries about her job but realizes the issue is more important than her own career.

stem cell research:

Stem cells are primal, undifferentiated cells that can become any type of cell in the body. Embryonic stem cells come from human embryos. The Church opposes embryonic stem cell research because it involves destroying early human life. The Church does not oppose adult stem cell research.

Bearing Fruit

Not everyone will face the same kinds of challenges that Julia Wagner did at Procter & Gamble. Most people will not have to argue to their bosses that it might actually be more profitable for them to leave unions in place rather than trying to undermine their efforts without regard to the company's cost. Small business owners certainly hope they will not have to lay off employees.

But being in business—whether as an owner, a CEO, or even a middle manager—places one in a position where these kinds of decisions can come into play. Some business leaders will defend practices such as remaining union-free as necessary for maintaining their businesses' competitiveness. When asked to enter into discussions of business ethics with church people, corporate captains often complain that the church lacks the necessary understanding of the business world. Defending a worker's right to strike is not exactly a popular stance in corporate boardrooms.

And yet listening to former Chiquita man Bob Ehrsam or Chicago business owner Gregory Pierce talk about their struggles to run successful businesses while keeping an eye on the moral tiller, one gets the impression that if you work hard enough at doing what is right, you will begin to see your efforts bear fruit. . . .

For Reflection

1. Many companies have mission statements that express their core values and goals. Make up your own company, or choose a real one. Briefly describe the company. Then write a mission statement for it that reflects the principles outlined in *Economic Justice for All*, including the threefold purpose of work.
2. Provide at least three examples of how people in the article "By Their Fruits You Shall Know Them" take action that reflects some aspect of *Economic Justice for All*. Use quotations from the readings to support your answer.
3. Which of the ideas in these readings do you think is most important for you to apply to your own work? Explain why.

Profile

Cesar Chavez

In 1965, California grape growers cut the wages of migrant farm workers during the grape harvest, prompting the workers to strike. Besides low wages, the workers had to endure inhumane conditions: toilets and fresh water were often inaccessible in the fields, and workers were constantly exposed to hazardous levels of toxic pesticides. Still, changing things by going on strike was a long shot; every previous farm workers' strike had failed.

This strike turned out differently, though, thanks in large part to the leadership of Cesar Chavez. Armed with a deep Catholic faith and a belief in the philosophy of nonviolence, Chavez had successfully organized twelve hundred families into the National Farm Workers Association (NFWA), which later became the United Farm Workers of America. When the grape harvesters decided to strike, the NFWA joined them.

Under Chavez's leadership, this strike took a different approach than previous ones. For one thing, it was firmly grounded in the spirituality of the workers: they held Masses, prayed, and marched under the banner of the Virgin of Guadalupe. Chavez extended that spiritual grounding by insisting on nonviolent tactics similar to those used by Gandhi and Martin Luther King Jr. Nonviolence meant that though the farm workers would march, picket, fast, and endure harassment, they would never use violence. Perhaps the most successful nonviolent tactic Chavez used was the grape boycott. Hundreds of the workers' supporters leafleted in front of grocery stores urging consumers to stop buying grapes until the growers settled with the workers. At its height, some seventeen million Americans participated in the boycott.

Thousands of the workers—including Chavez—were arrested for striking; hundreds of others were beaten or harassed, and three were murdered. But over many years, the farm workers won industry-wide labor contracts that provided humane working and living conditions for tens of thousands of people. And in 1975, California passed a law protecting the right of farm workers to unionize.

When Cesar Chavez died in 1993, more than forty thousand people attended his funeral. Others must continue his legacy, because even today, even in the United States, many workers continue to be denied basic rights.

Gustavo Gutiérrez

7

Economic Life

Introduction

Consider these facts: About half of the world's population lives on less than $2 a day, and some 25,000 people die of hunger every day, most of them children. How should the Church proclaim the love of God to people who live in such inhumane circumstances?

Ordinary Catholics in Latin America began gathering in small faith groups to reflect on that question beginning in the late 1950s. The answers that emerged from their reflection became known as liberation theology—a way of talking about God (theology) that focuses on God's desire for humankind to experience freedom (liberation) from every kind of suffering and death. Liberation theology proposes that because forced poverty is offensive to God and incompatible with God's Reign, Christians must stand with the poor and work to free them from poverty. The decision to make this a top priority is known as the preferential option for the poor.

The 1968 conference of Latin American bishops at Medellín, Colombia, greatly increased the influence of liberation theology in the Church. The bishops sharply criticized the injustices that cause widespread poverty in their society, and committed the Church to work with the poor to overcome those injustices. Medellín electrified the Church in Latin America. Religious sisters and brothers, priests, and lay leaders started getting more involved in the lives of poor people, who in turn began organizing to better support one another. Such activity met with violent resistance from those in power across Latin America.

Liberation theology was also challenged by some in the Church because of its reliance on Marxist social analysis. Catholic social teaching rejects several aspects of Marxism, including its claim that conflict between social classes (workers versus business owners, poor versus rich) is necessary, its denial of religious freedom, its denial of the right to own private property, and its limitation of individual freedom. Adding to Church leaders' concern was the fact that Marxist guerrilla groups were staging violent campaigns against governments across Latin America. The Vatican issued two documents in the 1980s that warned of Marxist influences on liberation theology. Those documents also noted that true liberation is more than freedom from poverty and oppression; ultimately, humans must be liberated from sin and death by the grace of God.

Although the Church has criticized the socialist and communist economic systems that emerged from Marxism, it has also been critical of unregulated capitalism, particularly its focus on maximizing wealth at the expense of human dignity and the integrity of the environment. As the United States bishops stated in their 1986 pastoral letter *Economic Justice for All*, "*Every economic decision and institution must be judged in light of whether it protects or undermines the dignity of the human person*" (no. 13). Any economic system that does not make room for solidarity, love, and justice falls short of that standard.

That is why, despite its limitations, liberation theology continues to influence Catholic social teaching. *Economic Justice for All* echoes some of the insights of liberation theology, as does the teaching of Pope John Paul II.

No one has done more to shape liberation theology than Gustavo Gutiérrez, a theologian and priest who spent much of his life working with the poor of Lima, Peru. The Latin American bishops incorporated many of his ideas into their Medellín documents, and his 1971 book, *A Theology of Liberation: History, Politics, and Salvation*, became the most influential text on the topic. It is excerpted in this chapter, along with part of a later book, *We Believe in the God of Life*. While Gutiérrez does not claim to have all the answers, his insights offer a way for the Church to better proclaim the Good News to those who live in poverty.

Excerpts from *Economic Justice for All: Pastoral Letter on Catholic Social Teaching and the U.S. Economy*

by the United States Conference of Catholic Bishops

Moral Priorities for the Nation

85. *The common good demands justice for all, the protection of the human rights of all.*[1] Making cultural and economic institutions more supportive of the freedom, power, and security of individuals and families must be a central, long-range objective for the nation. Every person has a duty to contribute to building up the commonweal. All have a responsibility to develop their talents through education. Adults must contribute to society through their individual vocations and talents. Parents are called to guide their children to the maturity of Christian adulthood and responsible citizenship. Everyone has special duties toward the poor and marginalized. Living up to these responsibilities, however, is often made difficult by the social and economic patterns of society. Schools and educational policies both public and private often serve the privileged exceedingly well, while the children of the poor are effectively abandoned as second-class citizens. Great stresses are created in family life by the way work is organized and scheduled, and by the social and cultural values communicated on TV. Many in the lower middle class are barely getting by and fear becoming victims of economic forces over which they have no control.

commonweal: the public good

86. *The obligation to provide justice for all means that the poor have the single most urgent economic claim on the conscience of the nation.* Poverty can take many forms, spiritual as well as material. All people face struggles of the spirit as they ask deep questions about their purpose

in life. Many have serious problems in marriage and family life at some time in their lives, and all of us face the certain reality of sickness and death. The Gospel of Christ proclaims that God's love is stronger than all these forms of diminishment. Material deprivation, however, seriously compounds such sufferings of the spirit and heart. To see a loved one sick is bad enough, but to have no possibility of obtaining health care is worse. To face family problems, such as death of a spouse or a divorce, can be devastating, but to have these lead to the loss of one's home and end with living on the streets is something no one should have to endure in a country as rich as ours. In developing countries these human problems are even more greatly intensified by extreme material deprivation. This form of human suffering can be reduced if our own country, so rich in resources, chooses to increase its assistance.

87. As individuals and as a nation, therefore, we are called to make a fundamental "option for the poor."[2] The obligation to evaluate social and economic activity from the viewpoint of the poor and the powerless arises from the radical command to love one's neighbor as one's self. Those who are marginalized and whose rights are denied have privileged claims if society is to provide justice for *all*. This obligation is deeply rooted in Christian belief. As Paul VI stated:

> In teaching us charity, the Gospel instructs us in the preferential respect due to the poor and the special situation they have in society: the more fortunate should renounce some of their rights so as to place their goods more generously at the service of others.[3]

> John Paul II has described this special obligation to the poor as "a call to have a special openness with the small and the weak, those that suffer and weep, those that are humiliated and left on the margin of society, so as to help them win their dignity as human persons and children of God."[4]

88. The prime purpose of this special commitment to the poor is to enable them to become active participants in the life of society. It is to enable all persons to share in and contribute to the common good.[5] The "option for the poor," therefore, is not an adversarial slogan that pits one group or class against another. Rather it states that the deprivation and powerlessness of the poor wounds the whole community. The extent of their suffering is a measure of how far we are from being a true

community of persons. These wounds will be healed only by greater solidarity with the poor and among the poor themselves.

89. In summary, the norms of love, basic justice, and human rights imply that personal decisions, social policies, and economic institutions should be governed by several key priorities. These priorities do not specify everything that must be considered in economic decision making. They do indicate the most fundamental and urgent objectives.

90. a. *The fulfillment of the basic needs of the poor is of the highest priority.* Personal decisions, policies of private and public bodies, and power relationships must be all evaluated by their effects on those who lack the minimum necessities of nutrition, housing, education, and health care. In particular, this principle recognizes that meeting fundamental human needs must come before the fulfillment of desires for luxury consumer goods, for profits not conducive to the common good, and for unnecessary military hardware.

91. b. *Increasing active participation in economic life by those who are presently excluded or vulnerable is a high social priority.* The human dignity of all is realized when people gain the power to work together to improve their lives, strengthen their families, and contribute to society. Basic justice calls for more than providing help to the poor and other vulnerable members of society. It recognizes the priority of policies and programs that support family life and enhance economic participation through employment and widespread ownership of property. It challenges privileged economic power in favor of the well-being of all. It points to the need to improve the present situation of those unjustly discriminated against in the past. And it has very important implications for both the domestic and the international distribution of power.

92. c. *The investment of wealth, talent, and human energy should be specially directed to benefit those who are poor or economically insecure.* Achieving a more just economy in the United States and the world depends in part on increasing economic resources and productivity. In addition, the ways these resources are invested and managed must be scrutinized in light of their effects on non-monetary values. Investment and management decisions have crucial moral dimensions: they create jobs or eliminate them; they can push vulnerable families over the edge

into poverty or give them new hope for the future; they help or hinder the building of a more equitable society. They can have either positive or negative influence on the fairness of the global economy. Therefore, this priority presents a strong moral challenge to policies that put large amounts of talent and capital into the production of luxury consumer goods and military technology while failing to invest sufficiently in education, health, the basic infrastructure of our society and economic sectors that produce urgently needed jobs, goods, and services.

93. d. *Economic and social policies as well as organization of the work world should be continually evaluated in light of their impact on the strength and stability of family life.* The long-range future of this nation is intimately linked with the well-being of families, for the family is the most basic form of human community.[6] Efficiency and competition in the marketplace must be moderated by greater concern for the way work schedules and compensation support or threaten the bonds between spouses and between parents and children. Health, education and social service programs should be scrutinized in light of how well they ensure both individual dignity and family integrity.

94. These priorities are not policies. They are norms that should guide the economic choices of all and shape economic institutions. They can help the United States move forward to fulfill the duties of justice and protect economic rights. They were strongly affirmed as implications of Catholic social teaching by Pope John Paul II during his visit to Canada in 1984: "The needs of the poor take priority over the desires of the rich; the rights of workers over the maximization of profits; the preservation of the environment over uncontrolled industrial expansion; the production to meet social needs over production for military purposes."[7] There will undoubtedly be disputes about the concrete applications of these priorities in our complex world. We do not seek to foreclose discussion about them. However, we believe that an effort to move in the direction they indicate is urgently needed.

95. The economic challenge of today has many parallels with the political challenge that confronted the founders of our nation. In order to create a new form of political democracy they were compelled to develop ways of thinking and political institutions that had never existed before.

Their efforts were arduous and their goals imperfectly realized, but they launched an experiment in the protection of civil and political rights that has prospered through the efforts of those who came after them. *We believe the time has come for a similar experiment in securing economic rights: the creation of an order that guarantees the minimum conditions of human dignity in the economic sphere for every person.* By drawing on the resources of the Catholic moral-religious tradition, we hope to make a contribution through this letter to such a new "American Experiment": a new venture to secure economic justice for all.

Endnotes

1. *Mater et Magistra,* 65.

2. On the recent use of this term see: Congregation for the Doctrine of Faith, *Instruction on Christian Freedom and Liberation,* 46–50, 66–68; *Evangelization in Latin America's Present and Future,* Final Document of the third General Conference on the Latin American Episcopate (Puebla, Mexico, January 27–February 13, 1979), esp. part VI, ch. 1, "A Preferential Option for the Poor," in J. Eagleson and P. Scharper, eds., *Puebla and Beyond* (Maryknoll: Orbis Books, 1979), 264–267; Donal Dorr, *Option for the Poor: A Hundred Years of Vatican Social Teaching* (Dublin: Gill and Macmillan/Maryknoll, NY: Orbis Books, 1983).

3. *Octogesima Adveniens,* 23.

4. Address to Bishops of Brazil, 6, 9, *Origins* 10:9 (July 31, 1980): 135.

5. Pope John Paul II, Address to Workers at Sao Paulo, 4, *Origins,* 10:9 (July 31, 1980): 138; Congregation for the Doctrine of the Faith, *Instruction on Christian Freedom and Liberation,* 66–68.

6. *Pastoral Constitution,* 47.

7. Address on Christian Unity in a Technological Age (Toronto, September 14, 1984) in *Origins* 14:16 (October 4, 1984): 248.

Excerpt from *We Believe in the God of Life: Gustavo Gutiérrez*

translated by Matthew O'Connell

We Believe in the God of Life

Victor and Irene Chero have been given a friendly introduction by Bishop Germán Schmitz, pastor of this area. Speaking in the name of the settlers in Villa El Salvador and of the shantytowns of Lima, they begin their greeting to John Paul II by saying: "Holy Father, we are hungry." The simplicity and frightfulness of these opening words set the tone for all that follows. "We suffer affliction, we lack work, we are sick. Our hearts are crushed by suffering as we see our tubercular wives giving birth, our children dying, our sons and daughters growing up weak and without a future." The reality of unjust and premature death is described in utterly unadorned language. Out of it comes, with renewed force, a profession of faith: "But, despite all this, *we believe in the God of life*." The lack of the necessities for living a human life is contrary to the will of the God whom Jesus reveals to us. A profession of faith in that God implies a rejection of this inhuman situation; conversely, this situation gives content and urgency to the proclamation of the God of life.[1]

> ### Villa El Salvador:
>
> An innovative, self-organized city located in the desert outside Lima, the capital of Peru, Villa El Salvador was created, without outside assistance, by the fifty thousand impoverished people who were forcibly resettled there from Lima in 1971.

The conclusion is unavoidable: "We struggle for this life in the face of death." This is the fundamental choice, and it is made over a period of time. "Necessity has compelled us to leave our distant villages, bringing with us a deep faith in God, and inspired by the longing for a more human life." Theirs is the faith of emigrants; they are driven by their understanding of God and their desire for a different kind of life. That is why they undertake their journey. God "is known through one's feet," as Carlos Mesters beautifully says, referring to the great biblical image of the journey or the way as a search for the God whom Jesus, the itinerant preacher of Galilee, reveals to us. That is what these settlers, too, are experiencing.

In the course of this journey they become a people: "In the recently formed communities, shared need has united and organized us; it has created among us a solidarity in the struggle for life and the defense of our rights." The determination to be in solidarity characterizes the life of the poor. At the same time, they declare that they are followers of Christ: "From the outset we have journeyed with the church and in the church, and the church has journeyed in us and with us." That is what the church is, a journeying amid a people: a people that becomes a Christian congregation, and a church that becomes a people on its way to God. These are two processes that support each other and retain their full vitality in Latin America, even if they stir uneasiness and even anxiety in some.

The Christian communities that are on the increase "among our believing and poor people" are seeking to carry on the mission that Jesus announced (see Lk 4:16–20): to proclaim the good news to the poor, with all that this good news implies. The two settlers speak their final words: "Holy Father, may your visit once again make the words of Jesus effective among us: 'Today, the prophecy you have just heard is fulfilled.' Then," say the two speakers emphatically, "our *hunger for God* and our *hunger for bread* will both be heeded." These two needs characterize the life of this people that is Christian and, at the same time, poor and oppressed. The voices of the poor repeat the message of Jesus at Nazareth; thus they bring the good news and evangelize all who hear them.

The waves of applause that ripple across the sea of human beings here present attest to the identification the hearers feel with the words of Victor and Irene. The man to whom they are speaking, John Paul II, is visibly moved as he listens. He answers: "I have listened very attentively to the words of your representatives—this family, this husband and wife— I have listened very attentively," he repeats, and then uses the language of Victor and Irene, "and have heard that there is a hunger for God, a hunger for God. This hunger is truly a treasure of the poor, a treasure that must not be lost." A fruitful, and not very common, pastoral dialogue has begun. The pope continues: "There is here a hunger for bread, there is here a hunger for bread." To this repetition the crowd answers "Yes, yes!"

This situation gives rise to a demand, and the pope continues, speaking forcefully: "Everything must be done to see to it that this daily bread is not lacking, for such bread is a right, a right expressed when we pray in the Our Father: 'Give us this day our daily bread.'" Prayer and commitment are inseparably connected. In hesitant Spanish as he looks for the right words and leaves brief silences, which only give greater power to what he says and to the solidarity he voices, John Paul II declares: "I want this hunger for God to remain, but I want the hunger for bread to be satisfied; I want means to be found to supply this bread. I want there to be none who go hungry for daily bread: people should be hungry for God but not starved for their daily bread." The doubly hungry multitude welcomes the assertion of these two rights with loud applause.

Hungry for God, yes; starved for bread, no.[2] Faith in God must lead to elimination of the lack of bread. The exchange I have just reported expresses this incompatibility with unparalleled vigor: faith and starvation cannot be combined, because the God of Jesus is the God of life, of all life. Because of their experience the believing poor grasp the point clearly, for their experience is the insider's experience of a situation of conflict, abuses, and injustice, which the Christian conscience must reject.[3] Otherwise, we take the name of the Lord "in vain," for that is what happens when we appeal to God in order to justify and induce forgetfulness of the mistreatment of the poor, or in order to evade the scandal of this mistreatment. The passages I have been citing help us avoid this danger and set us on the right road to the true God, the God of the kingdom, whom Jesus Christ proclaims to us.

Endnotes

1. Ten years ago, in Peru, when the living conditions of the poor were worsening and leading to hunger, exploitation, and unemployment, over a thousand pastoral workers signed a statement saying: "God shows himself to be the God who gives life, preserves it, defends it, rescues it from oppression, and makes it permanent in the risen Christ. We believe in the Lord and therefore we believe in life" (*Danos hoy nuestro pan de cada día,* Lima, November 1979).

2. No. 68 (April 1985) of *Páginas* is dedicated to this meeting in Villa El Salvador.

3. See Gustavo Gutiérrez, *A Theology of Liberation: History, Politics, and Salvation,* trans. Sister Caridad Inda and John Eagleson (2d ed.; Maryknoll, NY: Orbis Books, 1988). See also the Introduction to the second edition; "Expanding the View."

Excerpt from *A Theology of Liberation: History, Politics, and Salvation*

by Gustavo Gutiérrez

An Attempt at Synthesis: Solidarity and Protest

Material poverty is a scandalous condition. Spiritual poverty is an attitude of openness to God and spiritual childhood. Having clarified these two meanings of the term *poverty* we have cleared the path and can now move forward towards a better understanding of the Christian witness of poverty. We turn now to a third meaning of the term: poverty as a commitment of solidarity and protest.

We have laid aside the first two meanings. The first is subtly deceptive; the second partial and insufficient. In the first place, if *material poverty* is something to be rejected, as the Bible vigorously insists, then a witness of poverty cannot make of it a Christian ideal. This would be to aspire to a condition which is recognized as degrading to persons. It would be, moreover, to move against the current of history. It would be to oppose any idea of the domination of nature by humans and the consequent and progressive creation of better conditions of life. And finally, but not least seriously, it would be to justify, even if involuntarily, the injustice and exploitation which is the cause of poverty.

witness of poverty: choosing to live in poverty as an expression of faith

On the other hand, our analysis of the Biblical texts concerning *spiritual poverty* has helped us to see that it is not directly or in the first instance an interior detachment from the goods of this world, a spiritual attitude which becomes authentic by incarnating itself in material poverty. Spiritual poverty is something more complete and profound. It is above all total availability to the Lord. Its relationship to the use or ownership of economic goods is inescapable, but secondary and partial. Spiritual childhood—an ability to receive, not a passive acceptance—defines the total posture of human existence before God, persons, and things.

How are we therefore to understand the evangelical meaning of the witness of a real, material, concrete poverty? *Lumen gentium* invites us to look for the deepest meaning of Christian poverty in Christ: "Just as Christ carried out the work of redemption in poverty and under oppression, so the Church is called to follow the same path in communicating to others the fruits of salvation. Christ Jesus, though He was by nature God . . . emptied himself, taking the nature of a slave (Phil. 2:6), and being rich, he became poor (2 Cor. 8:9) for our sakes. Thus, although the Church needs human resources to carry out her mission, she is not set up to seek earthly glory, but to proclaim humility and self-sacrifice, even by her own example" (no. 8). The Incarnation is an act of love. Christ became human, died, and rose from the dead to set us free so that we might enjoy freedom (Gal. 5:1). To die and to rise again with Christ is to vanquish death and to enter into a new life (cf. Rom. 6:1–11). The cross and the resurrection are the seal of our liberty.

> **Lumen gentium:**
>
> the 1965 Vatican II document whose English title is *Dogmatic Constitution on the Church*

The taking on of the servile and sinful human condition, as foretold in Second Isaiah, is presented by Paul as an act of voluntary impoverishment: "For you know how generous our Lord Jesus Christ has been: He was rich, yet for your sake he became poor, so that through his poverty you might become rich" (2 Cor. 8:9). This is the humiliation of Christ, his *kenosis* (Phil. 2:6–11). But he does not take on the human sinful condition and its consequences to idealize it. It is rather because of love for and solidarity with others who suffer in it. It is to redeem them from their sin and to enrich them with his poverty. It is to struggle against human selfishness and everything that divides persons and allows that there be rich and poor, possessors and dispossessed, oppressors and oppressed.

> **kenosis:**
>
> Greek for "emptying"

> **poverty:**
>
> Gutiérrez is referring to voluntary poverty here—poverty that is chosen for the sake of a greater good.

Poverty is an act of love and liberation. It has a redemptive value. If the ultimate cause of human exploitation and alienation is selfishness, the deepest reason for voluntary poverty is love of neighbor. Christian poverty has meaning only as a commitment of solidarity with the poor, with those who suffer misery and injustice. The commitment is to witness to the evil which has resulted from sin and is a breach of communion. It is not a question of idealizing poverty, but rather of taking it on as it is—an evil—to protest against it and to struggle to abolish it. As Ricoeur says, you cannot really be with the poor unless you are struggling against poverty. Because of this solidarity— which must manifest itself in specific action, a style of life, a break with one's social class— one can also help the poor and exploited to become aware of their exploitation and seek liberation from it. Christian poverty, an expression of love, is solidarity *with the poor* and is a protest *against poverty*.[1] This is the concrete, contemporary meaning of the witness of poverty. It is a poverty lived not for its own sake, but rather as an authentic imitation of Christ; it is a poverty which means taking on the sinful human condition to liberate humankind from sin and all its consequences.[2]

Luke presents the community of goods in the early Church as an ideal. "All whose faith had drawn them together held everything in common" (Acts 2:44); "not a man of them claimed any of his possessions as his own, but everything was held in common" (Acts 4:33). They did this with a profound unity, one "in heart and soul" (ibid.). But as J. Dupont correctly points out, this was not a question of erecting poverty as an ideal, but rather of seeing to it that there were no poor: "They had never a needy person among them, because all who had property in land or houses sold it, brought the proceeds of the sale, and laid the money at the feet of the apostles; it was then distributed to any who stood in need" (Acts 4:34–35). The meaning of the community of goods is clear: to eliminate poverty because of love of the poor person. Dupont rightly concludes, "If goods are held in common, it is not therefore in order to become poor for love of an ideal of poverty; rather it is so that there will be no poor. The ideal pursued is, once again, charity, a true love for the poor."[3]

We must pay special attention to the words we use. The term *poor* might seem not only vague and churchy, but also somewhat sentimental and aseptic. The "poor" person today is the oppressed one, the one marginated

aseptic:

sterile or lifeless

proletariat:

the working class

from society, the member of the proletariat struggling for the most basic rights; the exploited and plundered social class, the country struggling for its liberation. In today's world the solidarity and protest of which we are speaking have an evident and inevitable "political" character insofar as they imply liberation. To be with the oppressed is to be against the oppressor. In our times and on our continent to be in solidarity with the "poor," understood in this way, means to run personal risks—even to put one's life in danger. Many Christians—and non-Christians—who are committed to the Latin American revolutionary process are running these risks. And so there are emerging new ways of living poverty which are different from the classic "renunciation of the goods of this world."

Only by rejecting poverty and by making itself poor in order to protest against it can the Church preach something that is uniquely its own: "spiritual poverty," that is, the openness of humankind and history to the future promised by God.[4] Only in this way will the Church be able to fulfill authentically—and with any possibility of being listened to—its prophetic function of denouncing every human injustice. And only in this way will it be able to preach the word which liberates, the word of genuine fellowship.[5] . . .

Endnotes

1. Although he is speaking in a somewhat different context, Régamey remarks with lucidity and realism that "the spiritual fullness of the Beatitudes does not replace its messianic meaning. . . . Christianity will always have the mission of taking on itself the hope of the poor. The task of the Messiah becomes the task of Christians. It is of utmost importance to maintain at the very core of the meaning of the Beatitudes their messianic significance. This must be translated to fit the changing circumstances which offer the challenge of fulfilling—according to Christ—the just aspirations of all persons, just as the Beatitudes announced the fulfillment of the just aspirations of the Jews twenty centuries ago" (*Le portrait spiritual de chrétien* [Paris: Les Éditions du Cerf, 1963], p. 26).

2. "Perfection, however, does not consist in the renunciation itself of temporal goods; since this is the way to perfection" (Thomas Aquinas, *Summa Theologica,* II-II, q. 19, a. 12).

3. "Lost pobres y la pobreza en los Evangelios y en los Hechos," *La pobreza evangélica hoy* (Bogotá: Secretariado General de la CLAR, 1971), p. 32.

4. The Mendellín document on "Poverty of the Church" distinguishes among three meanings of the term *poverty* and describes the mission of the Church in terms of that distinction. It might be useful to quote here the entire paragraph: "(a) Poverty, as a lack of the goods of this world necessary to live worthily as men, is in itself evil. The prophets denounce it as contrary to the will of the Lord and most of the time as the fruit of the injustice and sin of men. (b) Spiritual poverty is the theme of the poor of Yahweh (cf. Zeph. 2:3; Luke 1:46–55). Spiritual poverty is the attitude of opening up to God, the ready disposition of one who hopes for everything from the Lord (cf. Matt. 5:3). Although he values the goods of this world, he does not become attached to them and he recognizes the higher value of the riches of the Kingdom (cf. Amos 2:6–7; 4:1; Jer. 5:28; Mic. 6:12–13; Isa. 10:2 et passim). (c) Poverty as a commitment, through which one assumes voluntarily and lovingly the conditions of the needs of this world in order to bear witness to the evil which it represents and to spiritual liberty in the face of material goods, follows the example of Christ Who took Himself all the consequences of men's sinful condition (cf. Phil. 2:5–8) and Who 'being rich became poor' (cf. 2 Cor. 8:9) in order to redeem us.

    "In this context a poor Church:—Denounces the unjust lack of this world's goods and the sin that begets it;—Preaches and lives in spiritual poverty, as an attitude of spiritual childhood and openness to the Lord;—Is herself bound to material poverty. The poverty of the Church is, in effect, a constant factor in the history of salvation" (nos. 4–5).

5. In this regard it is necessary to rethink seriously the meaning of the assistance that the churches of the wealthy countries give to the churches of the poor countries. This assistance could very well be counter-productive as regards the witness to poverty that these poor churches should be giving. Moreover it might lead them into

a reformist approach, resulting in superficial social changes which in the long run serve only to prolong the misery and injustice which marginated peoples suffer. This assistance can also provide a satisfied conscience—at low cost—for Christians who are citizens of countries which control the world economy. In this regard see the famous article of Ivan Illich, "The Seamy Side of Charity," *America* 116, no. 3 (January 21, 1967): 88–91.

For Reflection

1. Summarize your understanding of liberation theology, including what it says about forced poverty and what it calls Christians to do.
2. How would your community be different if it fully lived out the ideas in these readings? Be as specific as possible in your description.
3. What statement in these readings do you find most challenging, and why?

Profile

The Catholic Worker: Embracing Voluntary Poverty

Gustavo Gutiérrez suggests that Christians ought to choose voluntary poverty as a style of life in order to be in solidarity with the poor. Choosing to live in poverty, he suggests, makes one fully aware of its evils—and more fully committed to eliminating it. But what might such a lifestyle look like?

One example can be found in Catholic Worker communities. The Catholic Worker movement got its start when Dorothy Day, Peter Maurin, and a few others first distributed copies of *The Catholic Worker* newspaper in New York City on May 1, 1933. Named for its audience (the Catholic working class), the paper was published to let people know the Church's proposals for creating a more just social order. From the beginning, Day, Maurin, and their friends put the paper's ideas into action by operating a bread line out of the newspaper office; later, they rented an apartment to shelter homeless women. That became the first house of hospitality, a place where those in need are treated as welcome guests—even as Christ in the disguise of a stranger. Soon, others began opening houses of hospitality in the spirit of the newspaper's program for social change. Today there are about 190 self-identified Catholic Worker communities in the United States and ten foreign countries.

Each one is different, but generally Catholic Workers live and pray together in community much as the first Christians did. Catholic Workers are committed to doing the works of mercy listed by Jesus in Matthew 25. Mike Sersch describes his experience living in a Catholic Worker house:

> Many times I have been asked what I do at Bethany House. A lot: laundry, cooking and baking, cleaning, writing, driving people to appointments, many little chores. But what all of us do most often is simply listening. Hopefully, with our hearts.
>
> Being at the Worker is to welcome those who are ignored into your life. Often in the midst of a hectic day, I must remind myself to sit down and listen to the person who is in front of me. Listening involves not just opening up my ears, but turning myself over to the pain suffered by a guest.

Such listening to "those who are ignored" is made possible by the choice of Catholic Worker volunteers to live as simply and as precariously as their guests—a sort of voluntary poverty. Although a life of voluntary poverty is not the same as being forced into poverty, this lifestyle enables Catholic Workers to work for justice in solidarity with those who have been ignored by society.

Craig Kielburger

8

The Political Community

Introduction

Two months before he died of cancer, Cardinal Joseph Bernardin received the Presidential Medal of Freedom, the nation's highest honor, from President Bill Clinton. As he placed the medal on the ailing cardinal's shoulders, Clinton praised him for fighting social injustice, poverty, and ignorance. "When others have pulled people apart, Cardinal Bernardin has sought common ground," the President said. "He has held fast to his mission to bring out the best in humanity and to bring people together" (*National Catholic Reporter,* Sept. 20, 1996).

The President's praise of the cardinal for bringing people together was especially remarkable given that Bernardin had spent many years speaking out on a wide range of issues that typically divide people into opposing political camps. For example, he was featured on the cover of *Time* magazine for the leadership role he played in the United States bishops' 1983 pastoral letter *The Challenge of Peace*, a document that was controversial for questioning U.S. policy on nuclear weapons. The same day he received the Presidential Medal of Freedom, he publicly criticized the President's welfare reform policy for abandoning the poor; three days later, he joined others on the steps of the Capitol building to protest Clinton's veto of a bill banning partial birth abortions.

Bernardin's eclectic mix of positions is rare in politics, but it was not random. His politics were guided by a consistent ethic of life, the principle that defending human life and dignity should be the priority that guides all aspects of public policy. Others (such as Eileen Egan) had proposed this concept before, but it was Bernardin who developed and popularized it in a 1983 speech. His consistent ethic of life has been widely adopted in Catholic social teaching. Most notably, it provides the framework for *Faithful Citizenship: A Catholic Call to Political Responsibility*, the document the United States Catholic bishops issue every four years in advance of the presidential elections.

Faithful Citizenship outlines key points of the Church's social teaching that ought to guide Catholics as they participate in the political process. Catholics who take the document seriously may end up feeling "politically homeless" because no single political party fully embraces the consistent ethic of life.

Many people suggest that religious people should "stay out of politics." In their view, religion is a private "me and God" affair that has no place in public life. Bernardin addressed this common argument in a speech he gave at Georgetown University on the same day he received the Presidential Medal of Freedom. In it, he defended the right of people to act on their religious values in their public life and proposed some ways they might do so.

Despite his sometimes controversial public stands, Bernardin was widely regarded as one of the most beloved figures in the United States Catholic Church. People in his Chicago archdiocese called him Cardinal Joe, or just Joe. When he died, on November 14, 1996, 100,000 people attended his wake, and thousands lined the streets to observe his funeral procession. Although he was deeply committed to the truth, he never used it as a weapon. In his 1996 Georgetown speech, he insisted that Catholics' public discourse be tempered by love, "a spirit of fairness, respect, restraint and a search for common ground" (*America,* Oct. 5, 1996). He was known for living that advice, which may be his greatest contribution to both the Church and the political community.

Excerpts from *Faithful Citizenship: A Catholic Call to Political Responsibility*

by the United States Conference of Catholic Bishops

Politics in this election year and beyond should be about an old idea with new power—the common good. The central question should not be, "Are you better off than you were four years ago?" It should be, "How can 'we'—all of us, especially the weak and vulnerable—be better off in the years ahead? How can we protect and promote human life and dignity? How can we pursue greater justice and peace?"

In the face of all these challenges, we offer once again a simple image—a table.[1] Who has a place at the table of life? Where is the place at the table for a million of our nation's children who are destroyed every year before they are born? How can we secure a place at the table for the hungry and those who lack health care in our own land and around the world? Where is the place at the table for those in our world who lack the freedom to practice their faith or stand up for what they believe? How do we ensure that families in our inner cities and rural communities, in *barrios* in Latin America and villages in Africa and Asia have a place at the table—enough to eat, decent work and wages, education for their children, adequate health care and housing, and most of all, hope for the future?

We remember especially the people who are now missing at the table of life—those lost in the terror of September 11, in the service of our nation, and in the bloody conflicts in Iraq, Afghanistan, the Middle East, and Africa.

A table is also a place where important decisions are made in our communities, nation, and world. How can the poorest people on Earth and those who are vulnerable in our land, including immigrants and those who suffer discrimination, have a real place at the tables where policies and priorities are set?

For Catholics, a special table—the altar of sacrifice, where we celebrate the Eucharist—is where we find the direction and strength to take what we believe into the public square, using our voices and votes to defend life, advance justice, pursue peace, and find a place at the table for all God's children.

Tasks and Questions for Believers

Our nation has been blessed with freedom, democracy, abundant resources, and generous and religious people. However, our prosperity does not reach far enough. Our culture sometimes does not lift us up but brings us down in moral terms. Our world is wounded by terror, torn apart by conflict, and haunted by hunger.

As we approach the elections of 2004, we renew our call for a new kind of politics—focused on moral principles not on the latest polls, on the needs of the poor and vulnerable not the contributions of the rich and powerful, and on the pursuit of the common good not the demands of special interests.

special interests:

Special interest groups are politically active in order to promote a narrow cause or agenda.

Faithful citizenship calls Catholics to see civic and political responsibilities through the eyes of faith and to bring our moral convictions to public life. People of good will and sound faith can disagree about specific applications of Catholic principles. However, Catholics in public life have a particular responsibility to bring together consistently their faith, moral principles, and public responsibilities.

At this time, some Catholics may feel politically homeless, sensing that no political party and too few candidates share a consistent concern for human life and dignity. However, this is not a time for retreat or discouragement. We need more, not less engagement in political life. We urge Catholics to become more involved—by running for office; by working within political parties; by contributing money or time to campaigns; and by joining diocesan legislative networks, community organizations, and other efforts to apply Catholic principles in the public square.

The Catholic community is a diverse community of faith, not an interest group. Our Church does not offer contributions or endorsements. Instead, we raise a series of questions, seeking to help lift up the moral and human dimensions of the choices facing voters and candidates:

1. After September 11, how can we build not only a safer world,

but a better world—more just, more secure, more peaceful, more respectful of human life and dignity?

2. How will we protect the weakest in our midst—innocent unborn children? How will our nation resist what Pope John Paul II calls a "culture of death"? How can we keep our nation from turning to violence to solve some of its most difficult problems—abortion to deal with difficult pregnancies; the death penalty to combat crime; euthanasia and assisted suicide to deal with the burdens of age, illness, and disability; and war to address international disputes?

3. How will we address the tragic fact that more than 30,000 children die every day as a result of hunger, international debt, and lack of development around the world, as well as the fact that the younger you are, the more likely you are to be poor here in the richest nation on Earth?

4. How can our nation help parents raise their children with respect for life, sound moral values, a sense of hope, and an ethic of stewardship and responsibility? How can our society defend the central institution of marriage and better support families in their moral roles and responsibilities, offering them real choices and financial resources to obtain quality education and decent housing?

5. How will we address the growing number of families and individuals without affordable and accessible health care? How can health care better protect human life and respect human dignity?

6. How will our society combat continuing prejudice, overcome hostility toward immigrants and refugees, and heal the wounds of racism, religious bigotry, and other forms of discrimination?

7. How will our nation pursue the values of justice and peace in a world where injustice is common, desperate poverty widespread, and peace is too often overwhelmed by violence?

8. What are the responsibilities and limitations of families, community organizations, markets, and government? How can these elements of society work together to overcome poverty, pursue the common good, care for creation, and overcome injustice?

9. When should our nation use, or avoid the use of, military force—for what purpose, under what authority, and at what human cost?

10. How can we join with other nations to lead the world to greater respect for human life and dignity, religious freedom and democracy, economic justice, and care for God's creation?

We hope these questions and the 2004 campaigns can lead to less cynicism and more participation, less partisanship, and more civil dialogue on fundamental issues.

partisanship:

strong support for a particular group, political party, or ideology, often accompanied by an unwillingness to listen to people with other perspectives or affiliations

ideology:

an organized system of beliefs and values that forms the basis of a social, economic, or political philosophy

A Call to Faithful Citizenship

One of our greatest blessings in the United States is our right and responsibility to participate in civic life. Everyone can and should participate. Even those who cannot vote have the right to have their voices heard on issues that affect their communities.

The Constitution protects the right of individuals and of religious bodies to speak out without governmental interference, favoritism, or discrimination. Major public issues have moral dimensions. Religious values have significant public consequences. Our nation is enriched and our tradition of pluralism is enhanced, not threatened, when religious groups contribute their values to public debates.

As bishops, we have a responsibility as Americans and as religious teachers to speak out on the moral dimensions of public life. The Catholic community enters public life not to impose sectarian doctrine but to act on our moral convictions, to share our experience in serving the poor and vulnerable, and to participate in the dialogue over our nation's future.

A Catholic moral framework does not easily fit the ideologies of

platform:

a statement of principles, priorities, and positions that guides a political party's actions

"right" or "left," nor the platforms of any party. Our values are often not "politically correct." Believers are called to be a community of conscience within the larger society and to test public life by the values of Scripture and the principles of Catholic social teaching. Our responsibility is to measure all candidates, policies, parties, and platforms by how they protect or undermine the life, dignity, and rights of the human person, whether they protect the poor and vulnerable and advance the common good.

Jesus called us to "love one another."[2] Our Lord's example and words demand care for the "least of these"[3] from each of us. Yet they also require action on a broader scale. Faithful citizenship is about more than elections. It requires ongoing participation in the continuing political and legislative process.

A recent Vatican statement on Catholic participation in political life highlights the need for involvement:

> Today's democratic societies . . . call for new and fuller forms of participation in public life by Christian and non-Christian citizens alike. Indeed, all can contribute, by voting in elections for lawmakers and government officials, and in other ways as well, to the development of political solutions and legislative choices which, in their opinion, will benefit the common good.[4]

In the Catholic tradition, responsible citizenship is a virtue; participation in the political process is a moral obligation. All believers are called to faithful citizenship, to become informed, active, and responsible participants in the political process. As we have said, "We encourage *all citizens*, particularly Catholics, to embrace their citizenship not merely as a duty and privilege, but as an opportunity meaningfully to participate [more fully] *in building the culture of life*. Every voice matters in the public forum. Every vote counts. Every act of responsible citizenship is an exercise of significant individual power."[5] Even those who are not citizens are called to participate in the debates which shape our common life. . . .

The Role of the Church

The Church is called to educate Catholics about our social teaching, highlight the moral dimensions of public policies, participate in debates on matters affecting the common good, and witness to the Gospel through our services and ministries. The Catholic community's participation in public affairs does not undermine, but enriches the political process and affirms genuine pluralism. Leaders of the Church have the right and duty to share Catholic teaching and to educate Catholics on the moral dimensions of public life, so that they may form their consciences in light of their faith.

The recent Vatican statement on political life points this out:

[The Church] does not wish to exercise political power or eliminate the freedom of opinion of Catholics regarding contingent questions. Instead, it intends—as is its proper function—to instruct and illuminate the consciences of the faithful, particularly those involved in political life, so that their actions may always serve the integral promotion of the human person and the common good.[6]

We urge our fellow citizens "to see beyond party politics, to analyze campaign rhetoric critically, and to choose their political leaders according to principle, not party affiliation or mere self-interest."[7] As bishops, we seek to form the consciences of our people. We do not wish to instruct persons on how they should vote by endorsing or opposing candidates. We hope that voters will examine the position of candidates on the full range of issues, as well as on their personal integrity, philosophy, and performance. We are convinced that a consistent ethic of life should be the moral framework from which to address issues in the political arena.[8]

For Catholics, the defense of human life and dignity is not a narrow cause, but a way of life and a framework for action. A key message of the Vatican statement on public life is that Catholics in politics must reflect the moral values of our faith with clear and consistent priority for the life and dignity of the human person.[9] This is the fundamental moral measure of their service. The Vatican statement also points out:

It must be noted also that a well-formed Christian conscience does not permit one to vote for a political program or an individual law which contradicts the fundamental contents of faith and morals. The Christian faith is an integral unity, and thus it is incoherent to isolate some particular element to the detriment of the whole of Catholic doctrine. A political commitment to a single isolated aspect of the Church's social doctrine does not exhaust one's responsibility towards the common good.[10]

Decisions about candidates and choices about public policies require clear commitment to moral principles, careful discernment and prudential judgments based on the values of our faith.

The coming elections provide important opportunities to bring together our principles, experience, and community in effective public witness. We hope parishes, dioceses, schools, colleges, and other Catholic institutions will encourage active participation through nonpartisan voter registration and education efforts, as well as through ongoing legislative networks and advocacy programs.[11] As Catholics we need to share our values, raise our voices, and use our votes to shape a society that protects human life, promotes family life, pursues social justice, and practices solidarity. These efforts can strengthen our nation and renew our Church. . . .

Endnotes

1. Cf. United States Conference of Catholic Bishops, *A Place at the Table: A Catholic Recommitment to Overcome Poverty and to Respect the Dignity of All God's Children* (Washington, DC: United States Conference of Catholic Bishops, 2002).

2. Jn 13:34–35.

3. Mt 25:40–45.

4. Congregation for the Doctrine of the Faith, *Doctrinal Note on Some Questions Regarding the Participation of Catholics in Political Life* (November 24, 2002), no. 1.

5. United States Conference of Catholic Bishops, *Living the Gospel of Life: A Challenge to American Catholics* (Washington, DC: United States Conference of Catholic Bishops, 1998), no. 34.

6. Congregation for the Doctrine of the Faith, *Doctrinal Note on Some Questions Regarding the Participation of Catholics in Political Life*, no. 6.

7. United States Conference of Catholic Bishops, *Living the Gospel of Life*, no. 34.

8. Cf. Congregation for the Doctrine of the Faith, *Doctrinal Note on Some Questions Regarding the Participation of Catholics in Political Life*, no. 4.

9. Ibid.

10. Ibid.

11. Resources designed to help parishes and dioceses share the message of faithful citizenship and develop non-partisan voter registration, education, and advocacy programs are available from the United States Conference of Catholic Bishops. For more information, call 800-235-8722 or go to *www.usccb.org/faithfulcitizenship*.

Excerpt from "The Public Life and Witness of the Church"

by Cardinal Joseph Bernardin

I. Religion and Politics: The American Style

The relationship of religion and politics is as old as the U.S. constitutional tradition. The nation was founded in great part by those who had experienced religious discrimination or who were wary of any close connection of religion and politics. Religious pluralism has been for this nation both a factual condition and a constitutionally protected characteristic of the society almost from its inception. Precisely because of its centrality to the U.S. political tradition, the issue of religion and politics requires constant intellectual attention.

Commentators have often noted an apparent paradox: Religion is kept strictly separate from the institution of the state, yet the U.S. public overwhelmingly thinks of itself as a religious people, with a very high percentage consistently affirming their religious convictions. The paradox is apparent because an argument can be made that careful distinctions between religion and politics may be in fact our source of religious vitality. I suggest we think of the role of religion in our society in terms of three questions: church and state, church and civil society and, finally, religion and politics.

Separating Church and State

The church-state question is the central structural element in understanding the role of religion in U.S. society. For all its centrality, however, it is actually a quite limited issue. It is best, I think, to try to keep it both limited in its significance and clear in its content.

The church-state relationship governs how the institution of the state will relate to religiously based institutions in our society. To discuss, debate, or analyze church and state is not at all to engage the

First Amendment:

The establishment clause of the First Amendment simply reads: "Congress shall make no law respecting an establishment of religion, or prohibiting the free exercise thereof."

exegete:

to interpret

Declaration on Religious Liberty:

a document of the Second Vatican Council that describes the right people have to practice their religion freely

full range of religious conviction, commitment and engagement in our society. The church-state relationship is narrow, juridical and institutional in character. Governed by the First Amendment to the U.S. Constitution, it essentially affirms that religious communities should expect neither special assistance from the state nor any discrimination in the exercise of their civil and religious activity in society. This description of the meaning of the First Amendment does not attempt to exegete the court decisions that address specific dimensions of the law. It is, rather, a political interpretation of this standard element of our constitutional life.

From the perspective of Catholic teaching, embodied in the "Declaration on Religious Liberty," the political meaning of the First Amendment is good law. It protects what the Second Vatican Council and Pope Paul VI asserted was the basic requirement of church-state relations in any culture: the freedom of the church. Keeping secular and religious institutions distinct in purpose and function, in fact, creates space for the church to teach, preach and serve. Having the freedom to function guaranteed by law allows the church—and any religious community in this society—to define its ministry, pursue its religious and civil objectives and demonstrate the transforming power of faith, love and grace in society.

It is precisely when the church-state relations are clearly defined in law that the second dimension of the role of religion in society becomes centrally important. The relationships, networks, institutions and associations that lie "beyond the state" are neither created by the state nor are they controlled by the state. The concept of civil society is captured in the distinction between state and society that is pivotal in the Western liberal tradition of politics and that both Jacques Maritain and

John Courtney Murray, S.J., used in building the case within Catholicism for the right of religious liberty.

Engagement in Civil Society

Both external and internal events in the United States have refocused scholarly attention and policy debates about the role and function of civil society. The collapse of Communism in Central Europe and the former Soviet Union has yielded proposals from the West on how "to shrink" the state and build the fabric of civil society. At the same time, troubling trends in the United States on issues as diverse as family life, education, citizen participation and general standards of civility have concentrated attention on the quality and character of our own civil society.

It is in the fabric of civil society that religious communities and institutions flourish. In terms of the U.S. political tradition, it is crucially important to stress that the logic of church-state relations, which lays stress on legitimate separation of secular and sacral institutions, should not govern the logic of civil society. The logic of this relationship is engagement, not separation. In other words, to endorse a properly secular state, which has no established ties to any religious institution, does not imply or mean that we should support a secularized society, one in which religion is reduced to a purely private role.

Both Catholic social theory and U.S. constitutional principles support a substantive role and place for religion in the fabric of our society and culture. The state will not and should not be the agent for advancing a substantive conception of religious values and principles in the life of the nation, but the state should not be hostile to the enterprise. Precisely because of the pervasive role of religious convictions among the citizens of our society, there is a legitimate place in our national life for these convictions to find expression.

Civil society is a sphere of freedom; it provides political and legal space for a multiplicity of actors and institutions to help form and shape the fabric of our national life and culture. In this sphere of freedom, religious institutions can exercise the full range of their ministries of teaching and service. Religious witness will only be as effective and as persuasive as the religious communities render it through the lives and work of their leaders and members. This is the meaning of being "free to function." We can demand this right; then we must meet our responsibilities.

While the constitutional framework that generates our place in civil society is clear enough, it is also clear that one finds in the debate about civil society today some voices that are less than comfortable with a vigorous role for religious institutions in our public life and policy debates. This may in part be due to the way some religious witness is undertaken. But it is also the case that some versions of civil society advance the logic of separation to the point where the public life of our society would lose its religious content.

If this happened, I submit, we would be a poorer culture and society. There is clearly no place for religious coercion or proselytism in our public life, but there is a broad area in which religious ideas and institutions can contribute to issues as diverse as strengthening the family, humanizing the drive of economic competition and defining our responsibilities as a nation in a very changed world.

Vision, Ministry and Citizenship

To those who are skeptical or simply opposed to a public role for religion, and to the community of believers upon whom lies the responsibility for religious witness, I submit there are three ways in which religious traditions can enrich civil society. The first is through religious vision and discourse. The Hebrew Scriptures tell us that, where there is no vision, people perish. A constant responsibility of religious communities is to enrich our public vision through the resources of ideas, values, principles and images that are the core of any great tradition.

In the Catholic tradition, I have tried to take the theme of the sacredness of the human person and develop its implications through a "consistent ethic" of life. The ideas supporting the consistent ethic have been cultivated in the Catholic moral tradition for centuries. But a convergence of forces arising from contemporary society threatens the sacredness of human life and creates a new context in which the ancient themes of an ethic of stewardship of life take on new relevance. Essentially, I have argued that we must systematically address a series of threats to life by building within civil society a shared vision of what human sacredness demands and how we install binding principles of restraint and respect in our personal codes of conduct and in our public policies.

The theme of a consistent ethic is only one way in which a religious tradition can enrich our public dialogue. I realize that part of the apprehension of some citizens, scholars and analysts is that religious convictions that are not universally shared will be thrust into our policy debates. I understand the concern, and I will return to it, but here I simply want to establish the point that a policy of excluding religious vision, discourse and insights from our search for coherent, just, viable public policies is a price too high to pay. Without vision, people perish; we need all the resources we can muster today in developing an adequate vision for our society.

But religion is not exhausted by ideas and vision alone. A second crucial contribution it can make to civil society is through the ministry and work of religious institutions of education, health care, family service and direct outreach to the poorest parts of our society. The web of religious institutions is a pervasive aspect of our social support system. I believe it is the time to think intensively about how a more extensive public-private pattern of collaboration could serve to extend the range of effectiveness of these institutions and at the same time use scarce public resources more efficiently in support of human needs.

Thirdly, perhaps the most effective, long-term contribution that religious communities make to civil society is the kind of citizens who are shaped, often decisively, by participation in a religious tradition. In Christian terms this is the link between discipleship and citizenship. Recent research, reflected in the work of Robert Putnam at Harvard University, as well as that of Jesuits John Coleman (see AM. 5/11) and David Hollenbach in the Catholic community, points to the way in which religious affiliation has a decisive impact on the kind of civic engagement of individuals, particularly engagement in the service of others.

In summary, my argument thus far has been in support of clear distinctions between church and state, in opposition to any exclusion of religion from civil society and in advocacy of a broad, deep, activist role for religious institutions in shaping our public life.

A Question of Style

There is a final piece of this argument, this one directed to the religious communities rather than civil society: the theme of religion and politics. My point here is that a proper understanding of both the logic of separation (church and state) and the logic of engagement (church and civil society) locates the church in the proper place for public witness. How religion engages the political order is a question of style, and style here carries major importance. Style refers to the way religious communities speak to the political process, and style also refers to the manner in which we engage others in debate and discussion.

One reason why some have apprehension about religious involvement in public life is the style sometimes employed by religious institutions or communities. My proposal, therefore, is that effective religious witness depends, in part, on our style of participation. Engagement in civil society must be characterized by commitment and civility; witness must be a blend of advocacy and restraint. I am hardly pressing for a timid or feeble religious voice! My concern, rather, is to establish from within religious communities standards of participation that will shape our public witness.

Allow me to use two examples. First, while I know there is a healthy debate on this topic among scholars, I am inclined to the view that our style of arguing a social position ought to distinguish among how we speak within the church, how we participate in civil society and how we address the state on law and policy. Within the church, the full range of biblical, theological themes that structure our belief should be used.

Within civil society, I also think that explicit appeal to religious warrants and imperatives is both legitimate and needed if we are to address some of the profoundly human themes that are at the heart of our policy debates. But when we address the state, I believe we should be

ascetic:

frugal or restrained

ascetic in our use of explicitly religious appeals. Here we seek to shape law and policy that will obligate all in society. At this point we accept the responsibility of making our religiously grounded convictions intelligible to those who do not share the faith that yields these convictions.

Secondly, our style of religious witness should constantly be a testimony to the theological virtue of charity, which, in turn, produces the civic virtue of civility. Vigorous pursuit of our deepest convictions— even those involving life and death—should not involve questioning the motives of others, or their character. We should vigorously oppose conclusions we find unwise or immoral; we should vigorously pursue objectives that are essential for human life and dignity. But we should also be known for the way in which our witness leavens public life with a spirit of fairness, respect, restraint and a search for common ground among contending positions.

CARDINAL JOSEPH BERNARDIN, archbishop of Chicago, delivered [this] address at Georgetown University, Washington, D.C., on Sept. 9, 1996, just hours before receiving the Presidential Medal of Freedom at the White House.

For Reflection

1. Drawing from *Faithful Citizenship* and Cardinal Bernardin's speech, describe the Catholic response to the argument that religion has no place in public life.
2. If politicians took Cardinal Bernardin's argument seriously, how do you think it would affect their campaigns, their activities in office, and their language? Cite specific passages from Bernardin's speech to support your answer.
3. What idea or statement in these readings do you find most challenging? What idea or statement do you find most inspiring? Explain why.

Profile

Craig Kielburger: Winning Freedom for Children

Craig Kielburger proves that you don't have to be a bishop or an elected official to participate in the political process. He was only twelve years old when he came across a story in the newspaper about a boy named Iqbal who had been murdered for speaking out against child labor practices. Kielburger was appalled at Iqbal's murder, and even more appalled to learn that Iqbal's experience of virtual slavery as a child worker was not uncommon.

After researching the issue of child labor, Kielburger persuaded friends from his seventh grade class to form a group called Free the Children. The group would work to end child labor and exploitation, but Kielburger and his friends also wanted it to "free the children" in another way—by empowering ordinary kids to act on an issue that directly affected them.

Kielburger and his friends began giving talks on child labor wherever they could; they knew their facts and spoke from the heart, quickly winning media attention and financial support. Soon Kielburger was touring South Asia to learn more about child labor firsthand.

While in India, Kielburger managed to wrangle a meeting with the Canadian prime minister, Jack Chrétien. During his trip, Kielburger had met hundreds of child laborers who did everything from making fireworks to disassembling used medical syringes—often under danger-ous conditions and the threat of abuse. He wanted to press the prime minister, who was leading a Canadian trade delegation, to raise the is-sue of child labor with the government of India. At first, Chrétien refused to meet, so Kielburger held a press conference with two boys recently freed from slave labor. Under public pressure, the prime minister agreed to the meeting. At first, he lectured the thirteen-year-old on the com-plexities of international trade. But Kielburger had done his homework and offered intelligent responses to the prime minister's objections. In the end, Chrétien agreed to raise the issue of child labor with the Indian government. It was the first of what would be many political victories for Free the Children.

Since its beginnings in 1995, Free the Children has grown to in-clude more than one million young people in some forty-five countries. In addition to educating people about child labor, Free the Children has helped prevent child labor by building hundreds of schools and health clinics. For his part, Kielburger, who has been nominated for the Nobel Peace Prize three times, continues to encourage young people to take action for justice. In addition to speaking around the world, he has writ-ten several books for young people and co-founded Leadership Today, an organization that trains youth leaders. To Kielburger, being young is no excuse for not changing the world.

Pope John XXIII

9

The International Community

Introduction

When the Soviet Union moved medium-range nuclear missiles to Cuba in 1962, President Kennedy vowed to block all Soviet ships until the missiles were removed—and to treat any attack from Cuba as an attack by the Soviet Union. As was later revealed, Soviet commanders in Cuba came much closer to actually launching the missiles than anyone realized at the time. At the height of the crisis, Pope John XXIII made a widely publicized radio address in which he called on the parties to exercise caution. According to some commentators, the Pope's intervention may have encouraged the Soviet leader to begin backing down the next day.

The world breathed a sigh of relief, but the Pope was deeply shaken by the Cuban missile crisis, and immediately set out to write an encyclical on international relations and peace. The result, *Peace on Earth (Pacem in Terris)*, was issued just six months after the crisis. The encyclical shunned the arcane language of diplomacy, with its emphasis on balances of power and deterrence, and instead talked about international relations in human terms.

The encyclical begins with a lengthy consideration of human dignity and rights, which later provides a framework for its discussion of international relations. The same moral law that governs relationships between individuals, the encyclical says, ought to govern relationships between states. It then outlines four values to be exercised by nations in the pursuit of peace: truth, justice, solidarity, and liberty. In this

states:

In the context of international relations, states are independent nations.

context, the Pope addresses the nuclear issue forcefully: "Hence justice, right reason, and the recognition of man's dignity cry out insistently for a cessation to the arms race. . . . Nuclear weapons must be banned" (no. 112).

Although *Peace on Earth* was warmly received, few global leaders have fully embraced its principles for international relations. One exception might be Kim Dae-jung, President of South Korea from 1998 until 2003. Frequently called the Nelson Mandela of Asia, Dae-jung spent decades fighting for democracy in South Korea, frequently at great risk to his life. One of those brushes with death led to his conversion to Catholicism; since then, Dae-jung has often commented on the influence his faith has had on his politics and policies.

When Dae-jung was finally elected to the presidency, improving relations with North Korea became one of his top priorities. The Korean War (1950–1953) had divided Korea into two countries. Communists ran a brutal totalitarian state in North Korea, while dictators ruled South Korea until democracy was introduced in the late 1980s. Although the two sides agreed to a cease-fire in 1953, hostilities never really ended; military forces on both sides were constantly prepared to resume the fight if provoked.

As president, Kim Dae-jung began what he called a sunshine policy toward the North, on the principle that warmer relations might achieve what a decades-long cold war had not. His policy reflects the spirit and principles of *Peace on Earth*, and although many in the West expressed skepticism, it has led to improved relations between the two countries. His efforts to establish peace with North Korea won Kim Dae-jung the Nobel Peace Prize in 2000.

Excerpts from *Peace on Earth (Pacem in Terris)*

by Pope John XXIII

80. With respect to States themselves, Our predecessors have constantly taught, and We wish to lend the weight of Our own authority to their teaching, that nations are the subjects of reciprocal rights and duties. Their relationships, therefore, must likewise be harmonized in accordance with the dictates of truth, justice, willing cooperation, and freedom. The same law of nature that governs the life and conduct of individuals must also regulate the relations of political communities with one another.

Our, We:

Prior to the papacy of John Paul I, the Pope referred to himself in the plural in official statements. Heads of state traditionally used the "royal we" because they spoke in the name of the whole people.

81. This will be readily understood when one reflects that it is quite impossible for political leaders to lay aside their natural dignity while acting in their country's name and in its interests. They are still bound by the natural law, which is the rule that governs all moral conduct, and they have no authority to depart from its slightest precepts.

82. The idea that men, by the fact of their appointment to public office, are compelled to lay aside their own humanity, is quite inconceivable. Their very attainment to this high-ranking office was due to their exceptional gifts and intellectual qualities, which earned for them their reputation as outstanding representatives of the body politic.

83. Moreover, a ruling authority is indispensable to civil society. That is a fact which follows from the moral order itself. Such authority, therefore, cannot be misdirected against the moral order. It would immediately cease to exist, being deprived of its whole *raison d'etre*. God Him-

raison d'etre:

reason for being

self warns us of this: "Hear, therefore, ye kings, and understand: learn, ye that are judges of the ends of the earth. Give ear, you that rule the people, and that please yourselves in multitudes of nations. For power is given you by the Lord, and strength by the Most High, who will examine your works, and search out your thoughts."

84. And lastly one must bear in mind that, even when it regulates the relations between States, authority must be exercised for the promotion of the common good. That is the primary reason for its existence.

An Imperative of the Common Good

imperative:

an obligation or duty

precept:

a rule or law

85. But one of the principal imperatives of the common good is the recognition of the moral order and the unfailing observance of its precepts. "A firmly established order between political communities must be founded on the unshakable and unmoving rock of the moral law, that law which is revealed in the order of nature by the Creator Himself, and engraved indelibly on men's hearts. . . . Its principles are beacon lights to guide the policies of men and nations. They are also warning lights—providential signs—which men must heed if their laborious efforts to establish a new order are not to encounter perilous storms and shipwreck."

In Truth

86. The first point to be settled is that mutual ties between States must be governed by truth. Truth calls for the elimination of every trace of racial discrimination, and the consequent recognition of the inviolable principle that all States are by nature equal in dignity.

Each of them accordingly has the right to exist, to develop, and to possess the necessary means and accept a primary responsibility for its own development. Each is also legitimately entitled to its good name and to the respect which is its due.

87. As we know from experience, men frequently differ widely in knowledge, virtue, intelligence and wealth, but that is no valid argument in favor of a system whereby those who are in a position of superiority impose their will arbitrarily on others. On the contrary, such men have a greater share in the common responsibility to help others to reach perfection by their mutual efforts.

88. So, too, on the international level: some nations may have attained to a superior degree of scientific, cultural and economic development. But that does not entitle them to exert unjust political domination over other nations. It means that they have to make a greater contribution to the common cause of social progress.

89. The fact is that no one can be by nature superior to his fellows, since all men are equally noble in natural dignity. And consequently there are no differences at all between political communities from the point of view of natural dignity. Each State is like a body, the members of which are human beings. And, as we know from experience, nations can be highly sensitive in matters in any way touching their dignity and honor; and with good reason. . . .

In Justice

91. Relations between States must furthermore be regulated by justice. This necessitates both the recognition of their mutual rights, and, at the same time, the fulfillment of their respective duties.

92. States have the right to existence, to self development, and to the means necessary to achieve this. They have the right to play the leading part in the process of their own development, and the right to their good name and due honors. Consequently, States are likewise in duty bound to safeguard all such rights effectively, and to avoid any action that could violate them. And just as individual men may not pursue their own private interests in a way that is unfair and detrimental to others, so too it would be criminal in a State to aim at improving itself by the use of methods which involve other nations in injury and unjust oppression. There is a saying of St. Augustine which has particular relevance in this

context: "Take away justice, and what are kingdoms but mighty bands of robbers."

93. There may be, and sometimes is, a clash of interests among States, each striving for its own development. When differences of this sort arise, they must be settled in a truly human way, not by armed force nor by deceit or trickery. There must be a mutual assessment of the arguments and feelings on both sides, a mature and objective investigation of the situation, and an equitable reconciliation of opposing views. . . .

Active Solidarity

98. Since relationships between States must be regulated in accordance with the principles of truth and justice, States must further these relationships by taking positive steps to pool their material and spiritual resources. In many cases this can be achieved by all kinds of mutual collaboration; and this is already happening in our own day in the economic, social, political, educational, health and athletic spheres—and with beneficial results. We must bear in mind that of its very nature civil authority exists, not to confine men within the frontiers of their own nations, but primarily to protect the common good of the State, which certainly cannot be divorced from the common good of the entire human family.

99. Thus, in pursuing their own interests, civil societies, far from causing injury to others, must join plans and forces whenever the efforts of particular States cannot achieve the desired goal. But in doing so great care must be taken. What is beneficial to some States may prove detrimental rather than advantageous to others.

Contacts Between Races

100. Furthermore, the universal common good requires the encouragement in all nations of every kind of reciprocation between citizens and their intermediate societies. There are many parts of the world where we find groupings of people of more or less different ethnic origin. Nothing must be allowed to prevent reciprocal relations between them. Indeed such a prohibition would flout the very spirit of an age which has done so much to nullify the distances separating peoples.

Nor must one overlook the fact that whatever their ethnic background, men possess, besides the special characteristics which distinguish them from other men, other very important elements in common with the rest of mankind. And these can form the basis of their progressive development and self-realization especially in regard to spiritual values. They have, therefore, the right and duty to carry on their lives with others in society. . . .

In Liberty

120. Furthermore, relations between States must be regulated by the principle of freedom. This means that no country has the right to take any action that would constitute an unjust oppression of other countries, or an unwarranted interference in their affairs. On the contrary, all should help to develop in others an increasing awareness of their duties, an adventurous and enterprising spirit, and the resolution to take the initiative for their own advancement in every field of endeavor.

The Evolution of Economically Under-developed Countries

121. All men are united by their common origin and fellowship, their redemption by Christ, and their supernatural destiny. They are called to form one Christian family. In Our encyclical

Mater et Magistra:

a 1961 encyclical by Pope John XXIII on social development

Mater et Magistra, therefore, We appealed to the more wealthy nations to render every kind of assistance to those States which are still in the process of economic development.

122. It is no small consolation to Us to be able to testify here to the wide acceptance of Our appeal, and We are confident that in the years that lie ahead it will be accepted even more widely. The result We look for is that the poorer States shall in as short a time as possible attain to a degree of economic development that enables their citizens to live in conditions more in keeping with their human dignity.

123. Again and again We must insist on the need for helping these peoples in a way which guarantees to them the preservation of their own freedom. They must be conscious that they are themselves playing the major role in their economic and social development; that they are themselves to shoulder the main burden of it.

124. Hence the wisdom of Pope Pius XII's teaching: "A new order founded on moral principles is the surest bulwark against the violation of the freedom, integrity and security of other nations, no matter what may be their territorial extension or their capacity for defense. For although it is almost inevitable that the larger States, in view of their greater power and vaster resources, will themselves decide on the norms governing their economic associations with small States, nevertheless these smaller States cannot be denied their right, in keeping with the common good, to political freedom, and to the adoption of a position of neutrality in the conflicts between nations. No State can be denied this right, for it is a postulate of the natural law itself, as also of international law. These smaller States have also the right of assuring their own economic development. It is only with the effective guaranteeing of these rights that smaller nations can fittingly promote the common good of all mankind, as well as the material welfare and the cultural and spiritual progress of their own people."

125. The wealthier States, therefore, while providing various forms of assistance to the poorer, must have the highest possible respect for the latter's national characteristics and timehonored civil institutions. They

must also repudiate any policy of domination. If this can be achieved, then "a precious contribution will have been made to the formation of a world community, in which each individual nation, conscious of its rights and duties, can work on terms of equality with the rest for the attainment of universal prosperity."

"Nobel Lecture"

by Kim Dae-jung

Distinguished guests,

I would like to speak to you about the breakthrough in South-North Korean relations that the Nobel Committee has judged worthy of its commendation. In mid-June, I traveled to Pyongyang for the historic meeting with Chairman Kim Jong-il of the North Korean National Defense Commission. I went with a heavy heart not knowing what to expect, but convinced that I must go for the reconciliation of my people and peace on the Korean peninsula. There was no guarantee that the summit meeting would go well. Divided for half-a-century after a three-year war, South and North Korea have lived in mutual distrust and enmity across the barbed-wire fence of the demilitarized zone.

Kim Jong-il:

the North Korean head of state

To replace the dangerous stand-off with peace and cooperation, I proclaimed my sunshine policy upon becoming President in February 1998, and have consistently promoted its message of reconciliation with the North: first, we will never accept unification through communization; second, nor would we attempt to achieve unification by absorbing the North; and third, South and North Korea should seek peaceful coexistence and cooperation. Unification, I believe, can wait until such a time when both sides feel comfortable enough in becoming one again, no matter how long it takes. At first, North Korea resisted, suspecting that the sunshine policy was a deceitful plot to bring it down. But our genuine intent and consistency, together with the broad support for the sunshine policy from around the world, including its moral leaders such as Norway, convinced North Korea that it should respond in kind. Thus, the South-North summit could be held.

communization:

the process of adopting communist principles

I had expected the talks with the North Korean leader to be extremely tough, and they were. However, starting from the shared desire to promote the safety, reconciliation and cooperation of our people, the Chairman and I were able to obtain some important agreements.

First, we agreed that unification must be achieved independently and peacefully, that unification should not be hurried along and for now the two sides should work together to expand peaceful exchanges and cooperation and build peaceful coexistence.

Second, we succeeded in bridging the unification formulas of the two sides, which had remained widely divergent. By proposing a "loose form of federation" this time, North Korea has come closer to our call for a confederation of "one people, two systems, two independent governments" as the pre-unification stage. For the first time in the half-century division, the two sides have found a point of convergence on which the process toward unification can be drawn out.

Third, the two sides concurred that the US military presence on the Korean peninsula should continue for stability on the peninsula and Northeast Asia.

During the past 50 years, North Korea had made the withdrawal of the US troops from the Korean peninsula its primary point of contention. I said to Chairman Kim: "The Korean peninsula is surrounded by the four powers of the United States, Japan, China and Russia. Given the unique geopolitical location not to be found in any other time or place, the continued US military presence on the Korean peninsula is indispensable to our security and peace, not just for now but even after unification. Look at Europe. NATO had been created and American troops stationed in Europe so as to deter the Soviet Union and the East European bloc. But, now, after the fall of the communist bloc, NATO and US troops are still there in Europe, because they continue to be needed for peace and stability in Europe."

To this explanation of mine, Chairman Kim, to my surprise, had a very positive response. It was a bold switch from North Korea's long-standing demand, and a very significant move for peace on the Korean peninsula and Northeast Asia.

We also agreed that the humanitarian issue of the separated families should be promptly addressed. Thus,

separated families:

Many people were separated from close relatives when Korea divided in 1953.

since the summit, the two sides have been taking steps to alleviate their pain. The Chairman and I also agreed to promote economic cooperation. Thus, the two sides have signed an agreement to work out four key legal instruments that would facilitate the expansion of inter-Korean economic cooperation, such as investment protection and double-taxation avoidance agreements. Meanwhile, we have continued with the humanitarian assistance to the North, with 300,000 tons of fertilizer and 500,000 tons of food. Sports, culture and arts, and tourism exchanges have also been activated in the follow-up to the summit.

Furthermore, for tension reduction and the establishment of durable peace, the defense ministers of the two sides have met, pledging never to wage another war against each other. They also agreed to the needed military cooperation in the work to relink the severed railway and road between South and North Korea.

Convinced that improved inter-Korean relations is not enough for peace to fully settle on the Korean peninsula, I have strongly encouraged Chairman Kim to build better ties with the United States and Japan as well as other western countries. After returning from Pyongyang, I urged President Clinton of the United States and Prime Minister Mori of Japan to improve relations with North Korea.

At the 3rd ASEM Leaders' Meeting in Seoul in late October, I advised our friends in Europe to do the same. Indeed, many advances have recently been made between North Korea and the United States, as well as between North Korea and many countries of Europe. I am confident that these developments will have a decisive influence in the advancement of peace on the Korean peninsula. . . .

The knowledge and information age of the 21st century promises to be an age of enormous wealth. But it also presents the danger of hugely growing wealth gaps between and within countries. The problem presents itself as a serious threat to human rights and peace. In the new century, we must continue the fight against the forces that suppress democracy and resort to violence. We must also strive to deal with the new challenge to human rights and peace with steps to alleviate the information gap, to help the developing countries and the marginalized sectors of society to catch up with the new age.

Your Majesty, Your Royal Highnesses, ladies and gentlemen,

Allow me to say a few words on a personal note. Five times I faced near death at the hands of dictators, six years I spent in prison, and forty years I lived under house arrest or in exile and under constant surveillance. I could not have endured the hardship without the support of my people and the encouragement of fellow democrats around the world. The strength also came from deep personal beliefs.

I have lived, and continue to live, in the belief that God is always with me. I know this from experience. In August of 1973, while exiled in Japan, I was kidnapped from my hotel room in Tokyo by intelligence agents of the then military government of South Korea. The news of the incident startled the world. The agents took me to their boat at anchor along the seashore. They tied me up, blinded me, and stuffed my mouth. Just when they were about to throw me overboard, Jesus Christ appeared before me with such clarity. I clung to him and begged him to save me. At that very moment, an airplane came down from the sky to rescue me from the moment of death.

Another faith is my belief in the justice of history. In 1980, I was sentenced to death by the military regime. For six months in prison, I awaited the execution day. Often, I shuddered with fear of death. But I would find calm in the fact of history that justice ultimately prevails. I was then, and am still, an avid reader of history. And I knew that in all ages, in all places, he who lives a righteous life dedicated to his people and humanity may not be victorious, may meet a gruesome end in his lifetime, but will be triumphant and honored in history; he who wins by injustice may dominate the present day, but history will always judge him to be a shameful loser. There can be no exception.

Your Majesty, Your Royal Highnesses, ladies and gentlemen,

Accepting the Nobel Peace Prize, the honoree is committed to an endless duty. I humbly pledge before you that, as the great heroes of history have taught us, as Alfred Nobel would expect of us, I shall give the rest of my life to human rights and peace in my country and the world, and to the reconciliation and cooperation of my people. I ask for your encouragement and the abiding support of all who are committed to advancing democracy and peace around the world.

Thank you.

For Reflection

1. What elements of *Peace on Earth* are reflected in Kim Dae-jung's "Nobel Lecture"? Cite specific passages from the readings in your answer.
2. How do you think the courage or fear of national leaders affects international relations? Draw on Kim Dae-jung's experiences to support your answer. What role might his faith have played in his decision to pursue a sunshine policy toward North Korea?
3. Pope John XXIII says that the same moral law that governs relationships between individuals should govern relationships between political communities (see *Peace on Earth,* no. 80). Guided by this principle, write a short letter to the international community providing your advice for how states might get along better. If you like, you can write the letter in the style of an advice column.

Profile

The Holy See: Using Diplomacy for the Good of Humanity

Besides being a religious organization with more than a billion members worldwide, the Catholic Church also has formal standing as a sovereign state among the community of nations. With fewer than a thousand residents, and with an area of just 108 acres, Vatican City is the smallest nation in the world. It was created through a 1929 treaty with Italy in order to preserve the freedom and independence of the Church after the Papal States (a territory ruled by the Pope) were absorbed into Italy. The Holy See, the Church governing body headed by the Pope, serves as the government of Vatican City. The Holy See maintains formal diplomatic relations with 174 sovereign states, is a member of numerous international organizations, and is a permanent observer at the United Nations; popes Paul VI and John Paul II both addressed the United Nations General Assembly.

Because the Holy See lacks the economic and territorial interests of other nations, it is in a unique position to promote human rights, peace, and the authentic development of impoverished nations. For instance, it signed the Nuclear Nonproliferation Treaty in 1971 to support efforts limiting the spread of nuclear arms, and it played a significant role in the collapse of communism in Europe in the 1980s.

Lindy Boggs, a former congresswoman from Louisiana, served as the first female U.S. ambassador to the Holy See from 1997 to 2000. In that role, she communicated U.S. foreign policy to the Holy See and fostered cooperation between the two governments on common goals.

"It's extremely busy," Boggs said of her work. "The Vatican is essential to the movements of peace and economic conditions of peoples of various countries. One of the major thrusts of the pope . . . was the forgiveness of Third World debt, and of course that included working with the World Bank and the International Monetary Fund and other departments of our government" (*Pittsburgh Post-Gazette,* April 23, 2001).

Boggs also mediated disagreements between the United States and the Holy See, such as the time the Pope visited Cuba against wishes of the United States. Ultimately, though, Boggs views her work in the context of her Catholic faith: "I don't think I would be in public service if it weren't for a feeling of being able to help all of God's children," she said. "It's about creating a better way of life for as many people as possible" (*Times Union* newspaper, November 7, 1999). The same could be said about the international diplomacy of the Church.

Walter E. Grazer

10

Safeguarding the Environment

Introduction

Could you imagine a world in which the Grand Canyon was dammed and flooded? or in which the bald eagle was extinct? or in which a chemical plant accident killed more than 18,000 people—and no one bothered to clean up the mess?

In fact, the government once planned to dam the Grand Canyon, until an environmental group drew public attention to the plans with a 1966 newspaper ad that read: "This time it's the Grand Canyon they want to flood. *The Grand Canyon*" (Environmental Movement History Web site). The bald eagle nearly did go extinct, with only 417 breeding pairs in 1963; fortunately, the eagle was saved through government protection and a ban on the chemical that was causing its decline (CNN.com Web site). And thousands of poor people died in Bhopal, India, as a result of a 1984 accident at a chemical plant owned by a U.S. corporation; more than twenty years later, the mess continued to cause illness and death among local residents (Guardian Unlimited Web site).

Events like these have fueled the modern environmental movement, which got its start in the late 1960s and early 1970s. The environmental crisis did not escape the Church's notice, either: "Man is suddenly becoming aware that by an ill-considered exploitation of nature he risks destroying it and becoming in his turn the victim of this degradation," Pope Paul VI wrote in 1971 (*Octogesima Adveniens*, no. 21).

Nevertheless, it has taken some time for the Church to develop its teaching on the environment. That is partly because Catholic social teaching focuses on protecting the life and dignity of the human person.

Drawing on the biblical command to "subdue" and "dominate" the earth (Genesis 1:28), Christians had traditionally viewed the environment as existing to serve people.

Though it is true that God intends people to use the earth's resources for the good of all, the Bible also refers to God's calling people to care for creation (see Genesis 2:15), and it contains numerous examples in which creation is valued simply because God made it (see Job, chapters 38 and 39, for instance). In recent years, the Church has begun to emphasize these points in its teaching about the environment. It has also pointed out that the good of every human person, now and in the future, is inextricably linked to the health of the environment. Respecting the life and dignity of the human person requires respect for the natural environment. John Paul II made these points in his message for the 1990 World Day of Peace, "The Ecological Crisis: A Common Responsibility." That was the first Church document devoted entirely to the environment; it influenced the United States Catholic bishops' 1991 pastoral letter *Renewing the Earth: An Invitation to Reflection and Action on Environment in Light of Catholic Social Teaching,* and prompted them to launch their Environmental Justice Program. The program's director, Walter E. Grazer, evaluated its progress in his 2004 article, "Environmental Justice: A Catholic Voice."

Most people would not want to imagine a world without the bald eagle or Grand Canyon or livable cities. Now, as the world faces even greater environmental threats, Catholics are challenged to draw on their spiritual heritage as they imagine the natural world they will leave for the next generation.

Excerpts from *Renewing the Earth: An Invitation to Reflection and Action on Environment in Light of Catholic Social Teaching*

by the United States Conference of Catholic Bishops

I. Signs of the Times

At its core, the environmental crisis is a moral challenge. It calls us to examine how we use and share the goods of the earth, what we pass on to future generations, and how we live in harmony with God's creation. . . .

Environmental issues are also linked to other basic problems. As eminent scientist Dr. Thomas F. Malone reported, humanity faces problems in five interrelated fields: environment, energy, economics, equity, and ethics. To ensure the survival of a healthy planet, then, we must not only establish a sustainable economy but must also labor for justice both within and among nations. We must seek a society where economic life and environmental commitment work together to protect and to enhance life on this planet. . . .

III. Catholic Social Teaching and Environmental Ethics

A. A Sacramental Universe

The whole universe is God's dwelling. Earth, a very small, uniquely blessed corner of that universe, gifted with unique natural blessings, is humanity's home, and humans are never so much at home as when God dwells with them. In the beginning, the first man and woman walked with God in the cool of the day. Throughout history, people have continued to meet the Creator on mountaintops, in vast deserts, and alongside waterfalls and gently flowing springs. In storms and earth-quakes, they found expressions of divine power. In the cycle of the seasons and the courses of the stars, they have discerned signs of God's fidelity and wisdom. We still share, though dimly, in that sense of God's presence in nature. But as heirs and victims of the industrial revolution, students of science and the beneficiaries of technology, urban-dwellers and jet-commuters, twentieth-century Americans have also grown es-tranged from the natural scale and rhythms of life on earth.

For many people, the environmental movement has reawakened appreciation of the truth that, through the created gifts of nature, men and women encounter their Creator. The Christian vision of a sacramen-tal universe—a world that discloses the Creator's presence by visible and tangible signs—can contribute to making the earth a home for the human family once again. Pope John Paul II has called for Christians to respect and protect the environment, so that through nature people can "contemplate the mystery of the greatness and love of God."

Reverence for the Creator present and active in nature, moreover, may serve as ground for environmental responsibility. For the very plants and animals, mountains and oceans, which in their loveliness and sub-limity lift our minds to God, by their fragility and perishing likewise cry out, "We have not made ourselves." God brings them into being and sustains them in existence. It is to the Creator of the universe, then, that we are accountable for what we do or fail to do to preserve and care for the earth and all its creatures. For "[t]he LORD's are the earth and its fullness; the world and those who dwell in it" (Ps 24:1). Dwelling in the presence of God, we begin to experience ourselves as part of creation, as stewards within it, not separate from it. As faithful stewards, fullness of life comes from living responsibly within God's creation.

Stewardship implies that we must both care for creation accord-ing to standards that are not of our own making and at the same time be resourceful in finding ways to make the earth flourish. It is a difficult balance, requiring both a sense of limits and a spirit of experimenta-tion. Even as we rejoice in earth's goodness and in the beauty of nature, stewardship places upon us responsibility for the well-being of all God's creatures.

B. Respect for Life

Respect for nature and respect for human life are inextricably related. "Respect for life, and above all for the dignity of the human person," Pope John Paul II has written, extends also to the rest of creation (*The Ecological Crisis: A Common Responsibility* [=EC], no. 7). Other species, ecosystems, and even distinctive landscapes give glory to God. The covenant given to Noah was a promise to all the earth.

> See, I am establishing my covenant with you and your descendants after you and with every living creature that was with you: all the birds, and the various tame and wild animals that were with you and came out of the ark (Gn 9:9–10).

The diversity of life manifests God's glory. Every creature shares a bit of the divine beauty. Because the divine goodness could not be represented by one creature alone, Aquinas tells us, God "produced many and diverse creatures, so that what was wanting to one in representation of the divine goodness might be supplied by another . . . hence the whole universe together participates in the divine goodness more perfectly, and represents it better than any single creature whatever" (*Summa Theologica, Prima Pars,* question 48, ad 2). The wonderful variety of the natural world is, therefore, part of the divine plan and, as such, invites our respect. Accordingly, it is appropriate that we treat other creatures and the natural world not just as means to human fulfillment but also as God's creatures, possessing an independent value, worthy of our respect and care.

By preserving natural environments, by protecting endangered species, by laboring to make human environments compatible with local ecology, by employing appropriate technology, and by carefully evaluating technological innovations as we adopt them, we exhibit respect for creation and reverence for the Creator.

C. The Planetary Common Good

In 1963, Pope John XXIII, in the letter *Pacem in Terris,* emphasized the world's growing interdependence. He saw problems emerging, which the traditional political mechanisms could no longer address, and he extended the traditional principle of the common good from the nation-state to the world community. Ecological concern has now heightened our awareness of just how interdependent our world is. Some of the gravest environmental problems are clearly global. In this shrinking world, everyone is affected and everyone is responsible, although those most responsible are often the least affected. The universal common good can serve as a foundation for a global environmental ethic. . . .

D. A New Solidarity

In the Catholic tradition, the universal common good is specified by the duty of solidarity, *"a firm and persevering determination* to commit oneself to the *common good,"* a willingness "to 'lose oneself' for the sake of the other[s] instead of exploiting [them]" (Pope John Paul II, *Sollicitudo Rei Socialis* [=SRS], no. 38). In the face of "the structures of sin," moreover, solidarity requires sacrifices of our own self-interest for the good of others and of the earth we share. Solidarity places special obligations upon the industrial democracies, including the United States. "The ecological crisis," Pope John Paul II has written, "reveals the *urgent moral need for a new solidarity,* especially in relations between the developing nations and those that are highly industrialized" (EC, no. 10). Only with equitable and sustainable development can poor nations curb continuing environmental degradation and avoid the destructive effects of the kind of overdevelopment that has used natural resources irresponsibly.

E. Universal Purpose of Created Things

God has given the fruit of the earth to sustain the entire human family "without excluding or favoring anyone." Human work has enhanced the productive capacity of the earth and in our time is as Pope John Paul II has said, "increasingly important as the productive factor both of nonmaterial and of material wealth" (CA, no. 31). But a great many people, in the Third World as well as in our own inner cities and rural areas, are still deprived of the means of livelihood. In moving toward an environmentally sustainable economy, we are obligated to work for a just economic system which equitably shares the bounty of the earth and of human enterprise with all peoples. Created things belong not to the few, but to the entire human family.

F. Option for the Poor

The ecological problem is intimately connected to justice for the poor. . . .

The poor of the earth offer a special test of our solidarity. The painful adjustments we have to undertake in our own economies for the sake of the environment must not diminish our sensitivity to the needs of the poor at home and abroad. The option for the poor embedded in the Gospel and the Church's teaching makes us aware that the poor suffer most directly from environmental decline and have the least access to relief from their suffering. Indigenous peoples die with their forests and grasslands. In Bhopal and Chernobyl, it was the urban poor and working people who suffered the most immediate and intense contamination. Nature will truly enjoy its second spring only when humanity has compassion for its own weakest members.

A related and vital concern is the Church's constant commitment to the dignity of work and the rights of workers. Environmental progress cannot come at the expense of workers and their rights. Solutions must be found that do not force us to choose between a decent environment and a decent life for workers.

We recognize the potential conflicts in this area and will work for greater understanding, communication, and common ground between workers and environmentalists. Clearly, workers cannot be asked to make sacrifices to improve the environment without concrete support from the broader community. Where jobs are lost, society must help in the process of economic conversion, so that not only the earth but also workers and their families are protected.

G. Authentic Development

Unrestrained economic development is not the answer to improving the lives of the poor. Catholic social teaching has never accepted material growth as a model of development. A "*mere accumulation* of goods and services, even for the benefit of the majority," as Pope John Paul II has said, "is not enough for the realization of human happiness" (SRS, no. 28). He has also warned that in a desire "to have and to enjoy rather than to be and to grow," humanity "consumes the resources of the earth, subjecting it without restraint . . . as if it did not have its own requisites and God-given purposes."

Authentic development supports moderation and even austerity in the use of material resources. It also encourages a balanced view of human progress consistent with respect for nature. Furthermore, it invites the development of alternative visions of the good society and the use of economic models with richer standards of well-being than material productivity alone. Authentic development also requires affluent nations to seek ways to reduce and restructure their overconsumption of natural resources. Finally, authentic development also entails encouraging the proper use of both agricultural and industrial technologies, so that development does not merely mean technological advancement for its own sake but rather that technology benefits people and enhances the land.

austerity:

thrift or self-denial

H. Consumption and Population

In public discussions, two areas are particularly cited as requiring greater care and judgment on the part of human beings. The first is *consumption of resources*. The second is *growth in world population*. Regrettably, advantaged groups often seem more intent on curbing Third-World births than on restraining the even more voracious consumerism of the developed world. We believe this compounds injustice and increases disrespect for the life of the weakest among us. For example, it is not so much population growth, but the desperate efforts of debtor countries to pay their foreign debt by exporting products to affluent industrial countries that drives poor peasants off their land and up eroding hillsides, where in the effort to survive, they also destroy the environment.

Consumption in developed nations remains the single greatest source of global environmental destruction. A child born in the United States, for example, puts a far heavier burden on the world's resources than one born in a poor developing country. By one estimate, each American uses twenty-eight times the energy of a person living in a developing country. Advanced societies, and our own in particular, have barely begun to make efforts at reducing their consumption of resources and the enormous waste and pollution that result from it. We in the developed world, therefore, are obligated to address our own wasteful and destructive use of resources as a matter of top priority.

The key factor, though not the only one, in dealing with population problems is sustainable social and economic development. Technological fixes do not really work. Only when an economy distributes resources so as to allow the poor an equitable stake in society and some hope for the future do couples see responsible parenthood as good for their families. In particular, prenatal care; education; good nutrition; and health care for women, children, and families promise to improve family welfare and contribute to stabilizing population. Supporting such equitable social development, moreover, may well be the best contribution affluent societies, like the United States, can make to relieving ecological pressures in less developed nations.

At the same time, it must be acknowledged that rapid population growth presents special problems and challenges that must be addressed in order to avoid damage done to the environment and to social development. . . . Even though it is possible to feed a growing population, the ecological costs of doing so ought to be taken into account. To eliminate hunger from the planet, the world community needs to reform the institutional and political structures that restrict the access of people to food.

Thus, the Church addresses population issues in the context of its teaching on human life, of just development, of care for the environment, and of respect for the freedom of married couples to decide voluntarily on the number and spacing of births. In keeping with these values, and out of respect for cultural norms, it continues to oppose coercive methods of population control and programs that bias decisions through incentives or disincentives. Respect for nature ought to encourage policies that promote natural family planning and true responsible parenthood rather than coercive population control programs or incentives for birth control that violate cultural and religious norms and Catholic teaching.

Finally, we are charged with restoring the integrity of all creation. We must care for all God's creatures, especially the most vulnerable. How, then, can we protect endangered species and at the same time be callous to the unborn, the elderly, or disabled persons? Is not abortion also a sin against creation? If we turn our backs on our own unborn children, can we truly expect that nature will receive respectful treatment at our hands? The care of the earth will not be advanced by the destruction of human life at any stage of development. As Pope John

Paul II has said, "protecting the environment is first of all the right to live and the protection of life" (October 16, 1991 homily at Quiaba, Mato Grosso, Brazil).

I. A Web of Life

These themes drawn from Catholic social teaching are linked to our efforts to share this teaching in other contexts, especially in our pastoral letters on peace and economic justice and in our statements on food and agriculture. Clearly, war represents a serious threat to the environment, as the darkened skies and oil-soaked beaches of Kuwait clearly remind us. The pursuit of peace—lasting peace based on justice— ought to be an environmental priority because the earth itself bears the wounds and scars of war. Likewise, our efforts to defend the dignity and rights of the poor and of workers, to use the strength of our market economy to meet basic human needs, and to press for greater national and global economic justice are clearly linked to efforts to preserve and sustain the earth. These are not distinct and separate issues but complementary challenges. We need to help build bridges among the peace, justice, and environmental agendas and constituencies. . . .

"Environmental Justice: A Catholic Voice"

by Walter E. Grazer

A new and distinctively Catholic voice on environmental issues has evolved over the last decade. It links traditional church teaching on creation, the common good, social justice and stewardship to major environmental challenges. This often overlooked development is found in initiatives in parishes, schools and other Catholic institutions across the country:

- In the Northwest, the bishops issued a major pastoral reflection on the Columbia River that offers a moral vision of pursuing the common good in the midst of polarization and conflict [see *America* 11/24/03, p. 13];
- In Florida, the dioceses are urging community-wide efforts to protect precious limited water supplies, especially the Everglades;
- In many Catholic hospitals, a new sense of environmental responsibility is shaping policy and practice;
- In the National Council of Catholic Women, local Catholic women's groups are addressing environmental health hazards and threats to poor children, like lead and asthma;
- In Washington, the U.S. Conference of Catholic Bishops is helping to shape the debate about how to balance a respect for private property and the demands of the common good.

This fall, the U.S. Catholic bishops' environmental justice program marks its 10th anniversary. The program responds to the environmental challenge of Pope John Paul II, notably his 1990 message, "The Ecological Crisis: A Common Responsibility." The bishops are seeking to create an authentically Catholic voice in the environmental debate, one that focuses on the human person's place in nature and that puts the needs of the poor and vulnerable front and center.

This new voice has old roots. The life of St. Francis of Assisi, for example, demonstrated a love for creatures and the poor that can inspire us to find a way to care for both the earth and the wretched of the earth. It is not surprising that Pope John Paul II declared St. Francis the patron of ecology. Many, including nonbelievers, see St. Francis as a source of inspiration. Too few, however, have reflected his love for both the poor and nature, but this is a distinctive feature of the bishops' pastoral letter "Renewing the Earth" (1991) and their statement "Global Climate Change: A Plea for Dialogue, Prudence and the Common Good" (2001). These documents offer moral principles, policy criteria and an ethic of responsibility and restraint as a foundation of a renewed environmental ethic in the Catholic community.

A Voice on Behalf of the Poor

Making the poor a priority is a defining element of the church's contribution to the environmental debate. The poor are vulnerable to environmental hazards. Poor families often live on the margins of society: in urban areas where their housing is poor, or in rural areas, where the land is overused, in flood plains or subject to drought. They often live near toxic dumps, where housing is cheaper. Some hold jobs that people of higher incomes would not consider, jobs that expose poorer workers directly to environmental toxins. In debates about the environment, the poor and vulnerable workers are often out of sight and have no voice.

In serving the poor, the Catholic community has increasingly focused on environmental justice. The Catholic Campaign for Human Development is helping poorer communities struggle with environmental health problems—pesticides, for example, that poison farm workers. Catholic Charities USA is training housing counselors to help low-income mothers learn how to protect their children from household toxic materials. Catholic hospitals and health care facilities are finding ways to lessen the harmful effects of medical waste treatment and to address health threats resulting from environmental damage.

The Catholic environmental commitment extends beyond the local community and includes global issues. In their statement Global Climate Change, the bishops insist we need not understand everything about the science of climate change to know it poses serious consequences for humans and the planet itself. Prudence calls for action on behalf of future generations, but the search for the common good is often overwhelmed by powerful competing interests and polarizing claims and tactics. In these struggles, the voices of the poor are missing. But their special needs must not be lost sight of as the richer countries struggle over the potential costs of climate change to their societies.

The Voice of Local Leadership

Environmental justice is everyone's responsibility, and stewardship for creation is every believer's duty. The bishops' program seeks to engage Catholics by helping them to integrate concern for the environment within the broader context of living their faith. The bishops are not urging an exclusive or narrow focus on the environment, but are seeking a way by which a community of faith can harness ethical values and everyday experience to live more in harmony with creation. This Catholic effort is assisted by the National Religious Partnership for the Environment, a remarkable interfaith collaboration of Protestant, Evangelical and Jewish leaders. The partnership helps each member community to pursue faithfully its own path and approach, while uniting to build a stronger voice for the larger religious community in environmental dialogue.

The integration of environmental concerns in the church's public agenda is making a difference around the country. As noted above, the bishops of the Northwest published a major pastoral statement on the Columbia River. Likewise, the bishops of New England and New Mexico have also issued pastoral statements addressing their communities' concerns with fisheries and water respectively. Efforts like these at the diocesan level help build local leadership, capacity and momentum.

The church often plays the role of convenor, pulling elements of diverse communities together to search for the common good. In Connecticut, for example, dioceses under the leadership of the Archdiocese of Hartford are building a coalition of civic, low-income and environmental groups to address urban sprawl and its impact on the community and land. In this instance, the church is playing a key role in helping the entire community face a critical concern. In the Mississippi delta, the Diocese of Houma Thibodeaux has brought together farmers, watermen and oil producers to address questions of pollution and coastal erosion.

Dioceses in Iowa and the National Catholic Rural Life Conference are helping local communities to face the negative environmental impacts of large-scale hog farming. Some Iowans are Catholics who own or contract to operate large hog farms. Others suffer directly from the air and water pollution generated by large-scale hog farming. Some have lost their small farms to larger corporate hog farms. The church is again playing an important role by convening the stakeholders to consider larger questions and consequences.

Major national Catholic organizations have joined forces in the Catholic Coalition for Children and a Safe Environment, which includes Catholic hospitals, Catholic Charities agencies, schools, women's groups and other institutions. They are addressing basic environmental health and safety issues, particularly as they affect children. This effort represents a major institutional commitment to deal with issues like asthma, lead, mercury and pesticide poisoning. And since the church owns collectively over 80,000 buildings, retrofitting or building new facilities that are more environmentally safe would be a major contribution by the Catholic community. Such retrofitting would substantially lower energy consumption and help maintain environmental health.

Three Challenges

Ten years into this effort, three significant challenges remain. Catholic thought and spirituality must continue to explore more deeply the unique place of the human person in nature and the larger web of life. Extremes need to be resisted. Some espouse an almost divine status for nature, without any reference to the unique dignity of the human person or the need for development. Others embrace a strictly utilitarian view of nature. The church, on the other hand, recognizes that humans are part of nature. It neither divinizes nature nor embraces a materialistic view. No environmental ethic will be satisfactory without a clearer perspective on the place of humans within nature and a better understanding of the moral responsibilities of caring for creation.

Second, the Catholic tradition of the common good and solidarity needs to be developed as an alternative to polarizing political arguments and special interests. Rather than having one side win and the other lose, concern for the common good refocuses our perspective on the need to move beyond special interests or narrow political motives to assume a common responsibility for the future of our planet.

Environmental stewardship is a fundamental exercise in solidarity. Our human responsibility begins with our appreciation of the basic goodness of other creatures. The earth is home to all creatures. Our charge is to live responsibly and use wisely the earth's resources and preserve its beauty, diversity and fecundity.

Third, the neglected needs of the poor have to take priority. The rhetoric of environmental justice must become real in policies, resources and priorities. We must find a way to give expression to the voices, needs and hurts of the poor and vulnerable if we are to integrate the search for social justice and environmental wholeness.

Since 1993, the Catholic bishops across the United States have been building a network of concern for the environment. The environment is an issue with a long-term horizon. While there is still much to learn after these 10 years, it is also necessary for us to recommit ourselves for the longer journey to make environmental justice an integral part of the lives of the members of the Catholic community. This effort, if fruitful, will express itself in our prayer and thought, our work and investments. We must all take to heart the challenge of Pope John Paul II that "today the ecological crisis has assumed such proportions as to be the responsibility of everyone."

For Reflection

1. How does Catholic theology and spirituality influence its approach to environmental justice? Cite at least three specific examples from the readings.
2. In your opinion, what are the three most important ideas or principles in these readings? Why are they important?
3. Evaluate your own relationship to the environment in light of the ideas and principles you named in question 2. In what specific ways do you live out those ideas and principles? How could you do better?

Profile

E. F. Schumacher: Imagining a Friendlier Economy

"At its core, the environmental crisis is a moral challenge" (United States Conference of Catholic Bishops, *Renewing the Earth*). Those words of the U.S. Catholic bishops neatly sum up the message of *Small Is Beautiful: Economics as if People Mattered*, a book that electrified readers with its vision of an economy that would respect both people and the environment.

When it was published in 1973, its author became a hero of the environmental movement practically overnight—and an unlikely hero, at that. Ernst Friedrich Schumacher (1911–1977) was not an environmental activist, but a well-respected economist who had trained and taught at Oxford University and served as an economic advisor to the British National Coal Board for twenty years. Moreover, his work was deeply rooted in his religious experience, particularly his interest in the economic influence of Buddhist principles and his long study of Catholic thinkers such as Dante, Pope Leo XIII, Jacques Maritain, and Thomas Aquinas. His studies eventually led to his conversion to Catholicism and formed the philosophical grounding for *Small Is Beautiful*.

Schumacher contended that modern Western economies are based on a materialist philosophy that values the production and consumption of material goods above all else. The problems that humanity faces cannot be solved as long as that is the case, he said:

> We shrink back from the truth if we believe that the destructive forces of the modern world can be "brought under control" simply by mobilising more resources—of wealth, education, and research—to fight pollution, to preserve wildlife, to discover new sources of energy, and to arrive at more effective agreements on peaceful coexistence. Needless to say, wealth, education, research, and many other things are needed for any civilization, but what is most needed today is a revision of the ends which these means are meant to serve. And this implies, above all else, the development of a lifestyle which accords to material things their proper, legitimate place, which is secondary and not primary. (*Small Is Beautiful*, p. 249)

In order to restore harmony between people and the planet, Schumacher said, economic decisions must place the good of people and the planet before the goal of maximizing profits or getting a good deal. *Small Is Beautiful* argued for the practicality of such an economy, and proposed how it might work.

Ultimately, Schumacher said, humanity will not solve its problems through science alone, but by drawing on the values of its religious traditions. Schumacher died four years after publishing *Small Is Beautiful*, but his ideas continue to be promoted by scholars and hundreds of grassroots organizations.

Dr. Martin Luther King Jr.

11

The Promotion of Peace

Introduction

Throughout human history, most people have believed that the only way to stop violence is through more violence: "Fight fire with fire," the old saying goes. Following World War II, that philosophy drove the United States and the Soviet Union to spend trillions of dollars in a race to have the most nuclear weapons. By the beginning of the 1980s, the two superpowers possessed nearly 54,000 nuclear weapons altogether—more than one million times the explosive power of the atomic bomb that killed some 140,000 people in Hiroshima. Despite that fact, each side continued to build more.

The United States' role in that situation prompted the U.S. Catholic bishops to speak out on the issue. Their 1983 pastoral letter, *The Challenge of Peace*, was controversial for its criticism of the nuclear arms race and its insistence that any first use of nuclear weapons would be immoral. But it achieved the bishops' goal of starting a national conversation about the morality of nuclear weapons. Ten years later, the bishops issued *The Harvest of Justice Is Sown in Peace*, a pastoral letter that revisits *The Challenge of Peace* in light of new insights and the end of the Cold War. Both documents summarize the Church's teaching on peace and how to achieve it.

That teaching has a long history. In the first few centuries of the Church, most Christians refused to fight in wars because it violated the example of Jesus, who died on the cross rather than resist violence with violence. But when the tribes of northern Europe began attacking the Roman Empire in the late fourth century, Saint Augustine argued that limited violent force might sometimes be justified in order to protect innocent lives. The principles of Augustine's just-war theory were further developed by other thinkers, including the great theologian Thomas Aquinas.

Although the just-war theory was intended to limit violent conflict, in practice it has often been ignored or misapplied. That has led the Church to encourage the use of nonviolent strategies for resolving conflict. It was the Hindu spiritual leader M. K. Gandhi (1869–1948) who, drawing on the Sermon on the Mount (see Matthew, chapters 5–7) and other sources, developed a systematic philosophy of nonviolence. More important, he proved the effectiveness of nonviolence by using it to win India's independence from the British empire.

Among the many people who were inspired by Gandhi's example was Dr. Martin Luther King Jr., a Baptist minister who became the most prominent leader of the U.S. civil rights movement. Like many people, King once believed that Jesus's command to "love your enemies and pray for those who persecute you" (Matthew 5:44) was not practical when it came to large social conflicts. How, for instance, were people of color to win basic civil rights when the white majority regularly used violence to maintain segregation? Gandhi helped King answer that question, leading King to use nonviolent strategies during the Montgomery bus boycott of 1955–1956. Previous boycotts had failed, but this one was successful. Despite that success, King found himself continually explaining and defending the principles of nonviolence, as he told students during a 1958 speech at the University of California at Berkeley, excerpted in this chapter.

People often use the word *peace* to mean the absence of violent conflict. King and other civil rights activists could have had that kind of peace by just going along with segregation. But they sought real peace, which the Church defines as the blossoming of justice and love in all human relationships. To find that kind of peace, people must stop turning to violence as the solution to their problems, and instead turn to Christ, who reconciles people with God and one another.

Excerpt from *The Harvest of Justice Is Sown in Peace: A Reflection of the National Conference of Catholic Bishops on the Tenth Anniversary of the Challenge of Peace*

by the United States Conference of Catholic Bishops

I. Theology, Spirituality and Ethics for Peacemaking

An often neglected aspect of *The Challenge of Peace* is the spirituality and ethics of peacemaking. At the heart of our faith lies "the God of peace" (Rom 15:33), who desires peace for all people far and near (Ps 85; Is 57:19). That desire has been fulfilled in Christ in whom humanity has been redeemed and reconciled. In our day, the Holy Spirit continues to call us to seek peace with one another, so that in our peacemaking we may prepare for the coming of the reign of God, a kingdom of true justice, love, and peace. God created the human family as one and calls it to unity. The renewed unity we experience in Christ is to be lived out in every possible way. We are to do all we can to live at peace with everyone (Rom 12:18). Given the effects of sin, our efforts to live in peace with one another depend on our openness to God's healing grace and the unifying power of Christ's redemption.

Change of mind and heart, of word and action are essential to those who would work for peace (Rom 12:2). This conversion to the God of peace has two dimensions. On the one hand, in imitation of Christ we must be humble, gentle and patient. On the other, we are called to be strong and active in our peacemaking, loving our enemies and doing good generously as God does (Lk 6:35–36,38), filled with eagerness to spread the gospel of peace (Eph 6:15).

Likewise, discovering God's peace, which exceeds all understanding, in prayer is essential to peacemaking (Phil 4:7). The peace given in prayer draws us into God, quieting our anxieties, challenging our old values and deepening wells of new energy. It arouses in us a compassionate love for all humanity and gives us heart to persevere beyond frustration, suffering, and defeat. We should never forget that peace is not merely something that we ourselves as creatures do and can accomplish, but it is, in the ultimate analysis, a gift and a grace from God.

By its nature, the gift of peace is not restricted to moments of prayer. It seeks to penetrate the corners of everyday life and to transform the world. But, to do so, it needs to be complemented in other ways. It requires other peaceable virtues, a practical vision of a peaceful world and an ethics to guide peacemakers in times of conflict.

A. Virtues and a Vision for Peacemakers

1. **Peaceable Virtues.** True peacemaking can be a matter of policy only if it is first a matter of the heart. In the absence of repentance and for-giveness, no peace can endure; without a spirit of courageous charity, justice cannot be won. We can take inspiration from the early Christian communities. Paul called on the Corinthians, even in the most trying circumstances, to pursue peace and bless their persecutors, never repaying evil for evil, but overcoming evil with good (Rom 12:14,17,21).

   Amid the violence of contemporary culture and in response to the growing contempt for human life, the Church must seek to foster communities where peaceable virtues can take root and be nourished. We need to nurture among ourselves faith and hope to strengthen our spirits by placing our trust in God, rather than in ourselves; courage and compassion that move us to action; humility and kindness so that we can put the needs and interests of others ahead of our own; patience and perseverance to endure the long struggle for justice; and civility and charity so that we can treat others with respect and love.

   "The goal of peace, so desired by everyone," as Pope John Paul has written, "will certainly be achieved through the putting into effect of social and international justice, but also through the practice of the virtues which favor togetherness and which teach us to live in unity."[1]

2. A Vision of Peace. A practical complement to the virtues of peace-making is a clear vision of a peaceful world. Thirty years ago Pope John XXIII laid out before us a visionary framework for peace in his encyclical letter *Pacem in Terris (Peace on Earth)*, which retains its freshness today. *Pacem in Terris* proposed a political order in service of the common good, defined in terms of the defense and promotion of human rights. In a prophetic insight, anticipating the globalization of our problems, Pope John called for new forms of political authority adequate to satisfy the needs of the universal common good.

Peace does not consist merely in the absence of war, but rather in sharing the goodness of life together. In keeping with Pope John's teaching, the Church's positive vision of a peaceful world includes:

a. the primacy of the global common good for political life,
b. the role of social and economic development in securing the conditions for a just and lasting peace, and
c. the moral imperative of solidarity between affluent, industrial nations and poor, developing ones.

a. *The Universal Common Good.* A key element in Pope John's conception of a peaceful world is a global order oriented to the full development of all peoples, with governments committed to the rights of citizens, and a framework of authority which enables the world community to address fundamental problems that individual governments fail to resolve. In this framework, sovereignty is in the service of people. All political authority has as its end the promotion of the common good, particularly the defense of human rights. When a government clearly fails in this task or itself becomes a central impediment to the realization of those rights, the world community has a right and a duty to act where the lives and the fundamental rights of large numbers of people are at serious risk.

b. *The Responsibility for Development.* A second element consists of the right to and the duty of development for all peoples. In the words of Pope John Paul II, "[J]ust as there is a collective responsibility for avoiding war, so too there is a collective responsibility for promoting development." Development, the Holy Father reasoned, will contribute to a more just world in which the occasions for resorting to arms will be greatly reduced:

[It] must not be forgotten that at the root of war there are usually real and serious grievances: injustices suffered, legitimate aspirations frustrated, poverty and the exploitation of multitudes of desperate people who see no real possibility of improving their lot by peaceful means.[2]

Development not only serves the interest of justice, but also contributes greatly to a lasting peace.

c. *Human Solidarity.* A third imperative is to further the unity of the human family. Solidarity requires that we think and act in terms of our obligations as members of a global community, despite differences of race, religion, or nationality. We are responsible for actively promoting the dignity of the world's poor through global economic reform, development assistance, and institutions designed to meet the needs of the hungry, refugees and the victims of war. Solidarity, Pope John Paul II reminds us, contributes to peace by providing "a firm and persevering determination" to seek the good of all. "Peace," he declares, will be "the fruit of solidarity."[3]

B. Two Traditions: Nonviolence and Just War

An essential component of a spirituality for peacemaking is an ethic for dealing with conflict in a sinful world. The Christian tradition possesses two ways to address conflict: nonviolence and just war. They both share the common goal: to diminish violence in this world. For as we wrote in *The Challenge of Peace*, "The Christian has no choice but to defend peace. . . . This is an inalienable obligation. It is the how of defending peace which offers moral options."[4] We take up this dual tradition again, recognizing, on the one hand, the success of nonviolent methods in recent history, and, on the other, the increasing disorder of the post–Cold War world with its pressures for limited military engagement and humanitarian intervention.

Throughout history there has been a shifting relation between the two streams of the tradition which always remain in tension. Like Christians before us who have sought to read the signs of the times in light of this dual tradition, we today struggle to assess the lessons of the nonviolent revolutions in Eastern Europe in 1989 and the former Soviet Union in 1991, on the one hand, and of the conflicts in Central America, the Persian Gulf, Bosnia, Somalia, Lebanon, Cambodia, and Northern Ireland on the other.

nonviolent revolutions:

In 1989, nonviolent protests by thousands of people brought a peaceful end to communism in Eastern Europe.

The devastation wrought by these recent wars reinforces and strengthens for us the strong presumption against the use of force, which is shared by both traditions. Overall, the wars fought in the last fifty years show a dramatic rise in the proportion of noncombatant casualties. This fact points to the need for clear moral restraints both in avoiding war and in limiting its consequences. The high level of civilian deaths raises serious moral questions about the political choices and military doctrines which have had such tragic results over the last half century. The presumption against the use of force has also been strengthened by the examples of the effectiveness of nonviolence in some places in Eastern Europe and elsewhere.

Our conference's approach, as outlined in *The Challenge of Peace*, can be summarized in this way:

1. In situations of conflict, our constant commitment ought to be, as far as possible, to strive for justice through nonviolent means.
2. But, when sustained attempts at nonviolent action fail to protect the innocent against fundamental injustice, then legitimate political authorities are permitted as a last resort to employ limited force to rescue the innocent and establish justice.

Despite areas of convergence between a nonviolent ethic and a just-war ethic, however, we acknowledge the diverse perspectives within our Church on the validity of the use of force. Many believe just-war thinking remains valid because it recognizes that force may be necessary in a sinful world, even as it restrains war by placing strict moral limits on when, why and how this force may be used. Others object in principle to the use of force, and these principled objections to the just-war tradition are sometimes joined with other criticisms that just-war criteria have been ineffective in preventing unjust acts of war in recent decades and that these criteria cannot be satisfied under the conditions of modern warfare.

Likewise, there are diverse points of view within the Catholic community on the moral meaning and efficacy of a total commitment to nonviolence in an unjust world. Clearly some believe that a full commitment to nonviolence best reflects the Gospel commitment to peace.

Others argue that such an approach ignores the reality of grave evil in the world and avoids the moral responsibility to actively resist and confront injustice with military force if other means fail. Both the just-war and nonviolent traditions offer significant moral insight, but continue to face difficult tests in a world marked by so much violence and injustice. Acknowledging this diversity of opinion, we reaffirm the Church's traditional teaching on the ethical conditions for the use of force by public authority.

Ten years after our pastoral letter, recent events raise new questions and concerns which need to be addressed:

1. **Nonviolence: New Importance.** As *The Challenge of Peace* observed, "The vision of Christian nonviolence is not passive about injustice and the defense of the rights of others."[5] It ought not be confused with popular notions of nonresisting pacifism. For it consists of a commitment to resist manifest injustice and public evil with means other than force. These include dialogue, negotiations, protests, strikes, boycotts, civil disobedience, and civilian resistance. Although nonviolence has often been regarded as simply a personal option or vocation, recent history suggests that in some circumstances it can be an effective public undertaking as well. Dramatic political transitions in places as diverse as the Philippines and Eastern Europe demonstrate the power of nonviolent action, even against dictatorial and totalitarian regimes. Writing about the events of 1989, Pope John Paul II said,

> **European order:**
>
> After World War II, totalitarian communism dominated Eastern Europe.

It seemed that the European order resulting from the Second World War . . . could only be overturned by another war. Instead, it has been overcome by the nonviolent commitment of people who, while always refusing to yield to the force of power, succeeded time after time in finding effective ways of bearing witness to the truth.[6]

These nonviolent revolutions challenge us to find ways to take into full account the power of organized, active nonviolence. What is the real potential power of serious nonviolent strategies and tactics—and their limits? What are the ethical requirements when organized nonviolence fails to overcome evil and when totalitarian powers inflict massive injustice on an entire people? What are the responsibilities of and limits on the international community? One must ask, in light of recent history, whether nonviolence should be restricted to personal commitments or whether it also should have a place in the public order with the tradition of justified and limited war. National leaders bear a moral obligation to see that nonviolent alternatives are seriously considered for dealing with conflicts. New styles of preventative diplomacy and conflict resolution ought to be explored, tried, improved, and supported. As a nation we should promote research, education and training in nonviolent means of resisting evil. Nonviolent strategies need greater attention in international affairs.

Such obligations do not detract from a state's right and duty to defend against aggression as a last resort. They do, however, raise the threshold for the recourse to force by establishing institutions which promote nonviolent solutions of disputes and nurturing political commitment to such efforts. In some future conflicts, strikes and people power could be more effective than guns and bullets.

2. **Just War: New Questions.** The just-war tradition consists of a body of ethical reflection on the justifiable use of force. In the interest of overcoming injustice, reducing violence, and preventing its expansion, the tradition aims at:

- clarifying when force may be used,
- limiting the resort to force, and
- restraining damage done by military forces during war.

The just-war tradition begins with a strong presumption against the use of force and then establishes the conditions when this presumption may be overridden for the sake of preserving the kind of peace which protects human dignity and human rights.

In a disordered world, where peaceful resolution of conflicts sometimes fails, the just-war tradition provides an important moral framework for restraining and regulating the limited use of force by governments and international organizations. Since the just-war tradition is often misunderstood or selectively applied, we summarize its major components, which are drawn from traditional Catholic teaching.

First, whether lethal force may be used is governed by the following criteria:

- *Just Cause:* force may be used only to correct a grave, public evil, i.e., aggression or massive violation of the basic rights of whole populations;
- *Comparative Justice:* while there may be rights and wrongs on all sides of a conflict, to override the presumption against the use of force the injustice suffered by one party must significantly outweigh that suffered by the other;
- *Legitimate Authority:* only duly constituted public authorities may use deadly force or wage war;
- *Right Intention:* force may be used only in a truly just cause and solely for that purpose;
- *Probability of Success:* arms may not be used in a futile cause or in a case where disproportionate measures are required to achieve success;
- *Proportionality:* the overall destruction expected from the use of force must be outweighed by the good to be achieved;
- *Last Resort:* force may be used only after all peaceful alternatives have been seriously tried and exhausted.

These criteria *(jus ad bellum),* taken as a whole, must be satisfied in order to override the strong presumption against the use of force. Second, the just-war tradition seeks also to curb the violence of war through restraint on armed combat between the contending parties by imposing the following moral standards *(jus in bello)* for the conduct of armed conflict:

- *Noncombatant Immunity:* civilians may not be the object of direct attack, and military personnel must take due care to avoid and minimize indirect harm to civilians;

jus ad bellum:

Latin for "justice toward war"

jus in bello:

Latin for "justice in war"

- *Proportionality:* in the conduct of hostilities, efforts must be made to attain military objectives with no more force than is militarily necessary and to avoid disproportionate collateral damage to civilian life and property;
- *Right Intention:* even in the midst of conflict, the aim of political and military leaders must be peace with justice, so that acts of vengeance and indiscriminate violence, whether by individuals, military units or governments, are forbidden.

During the last decade, there has been increasing focus on the moral questions raised by the just-war tradition and its application to specific uses of force. We welcome this renewed attention and hope our own efforts have contributed to this dialogue. We also recognize that the application of these principles requires the exercise of the virtue of prudence; people of good will may differ on specific conclusions. The just-war tradition is not a weapon to be used to justify a political conclusion or a set of mechanical criteria that automatically yields a simple answer, but a way of moral reasoning to discern the ethical limits of action. Policy-makers, advocates and opponents of the use of force need to be careful not to apply the tradition selectively, simply to justify their own positions. Likewise, any application of just-war principles depends on the availability of accurate information not easily obtained in the pressured political context in which such choices must be made.

The just-war tradition has attained growing influence on political deliberations on the use of force and in some forms of military training. Just-war norms helped shape public debate prior to the Gulf War. In addition, the military's call for civilian leaders to define carefully objectives for the use of force is in keeping with the spirit of the tradition. At the same time, some contemporary strategies and practices seem to raise serious questions when seen in the light of strict just-war analysis.

For example, strategies calling for use of overwhelming and decisive force can raise issues of proportionality and discrimination. Strategies and tactics that lead to avoidable casualties are inconsistent with the underlying intention of the just-war tradition of limiting the destructiveness of armed conflict. Efforts to reduce the risk to a nation's own forces must be limited by careful judgments of military necessity so as not to neglect the rights of civilians and armed adversaries.

In light of the preeminent place of air power in today's military doctrine, more reflection is needed on how traditional ethical restraints should be applied to the use of air forces. For example, the targeting of civilian infrastructure, which afflicts ordinary citizens long after hostilities have ceased, can amount to making war on noncombatants rather than against opposing armies. Fifty years after Coventry, Dresden, Hamburg, Hiroshima, and Nagasaki, ways must be found to apply standards of proportionality and noncombatant immunity in a meaningful way to air warfare.

Moral reflection on the use of force calls for a spirit of moderation rare in contemporary political culture. The increasing violence of our society, its growing insensitivity to the sacredness of life, and the glorification of the technology of destruction in popular culture could inevitably impair our society's ability to apply just-war criteria honestly and effectively in time of crisis.

In the absence of a commitment of respect for life and a culture of restraint, it will not be easy to apply the just-war tradition, not just as a set of ideas, but as a system of effective social constraints on the use of force. There is need for greater public understanding of just-war criteria and greater efforts to apply just-war restraints in political decision making and military planning, training and command systems and public debate.

Ten years after *The Challenge of Peace*, given the neglect of peaceable virtues and the destructiveness of today's weaponry, serious questions still remain about whether modern war in all its savagery can meet the hard tests set by the just-war tradition. Important work needs to be done in refining, clarifying, and applying the just-war tradition to the choices facing our decision makers in this still violent and dangerous world.

Endnotes

1. John Paul II, *On Social Concern (Sollicitudo Rei Socialis)*, papal encyclical (Washington, DC: United States Catholic Conference, 1987), no. 39.

2. John Paul II, *On the Hundredth Anniversary of Rerum Novarum (Centesimus Annus)*, papal encyclical (Washington, DC: United States Catholic Conference, 1991), no. 52.

3. *On Social Concern,* nos. 38, 39.

4. National Conference of Catholic Bishops, *The Challenge of Peace* (Washington, DC: United States Catholic Conference, 1983), no. 73.

5. Ibid., no. 116.

6. *On the Hundredth Anniversary of Rerum Novarum*, no. 23.

Excerpt from *I Have a Dream: Writings and Speeches That Changed the World*

by Martin Luther King Jr.

The Power of Nonviolence (1958)

From the very beginning there was a philosophy undergirding the Montgomery boycott, the philosophy of nonviolent resistance. There was always the problem of getting this method over because it didn't make sense to most of the people in the beginning. We had to use our mass meetings to explain nonviolence to a community of people who had never heard of the philosophy and in many instances were not sympathetic with it. We had meetings twice a week on Mondays and on Thursdays, and we had an institute on nonviolence and social change: We had to make it clear that nonviolent resistance is not a method of cowardice. It does resist. It is not a method of stagnant passivity and deadening complacency. The nonviolent resister is just as opposed to the evil that he is standing against as the violent resister but he resists without violence. This method is nonaggressive physically but strongly aggressive spiritually.

> **Montgomery boycott:**
>
> the black boycott of city buses in Montgomery, Alabama, from December 1955 to December 1956

Not to Humiliate but to Win Over

Another thing that we had to get over was the fact that the nonviolent resister does not seek to humiliate or defeat the opponent but to win his friendship and understanding. This was always a cry that we had to set before people that our aim is not to defeat the white community, not to humiliate the white community, but to win the friendship of all of the persons who had perpetrated this system in the past. The end of violence or the aftermath of violence is bitterness. The aftermath of nonviolence is reconciliation and the creation of a beloved community. A boycott is never an end within itself. It is merely a means to awaken a sense of shame within the oppressor but the end is reconciliation, the end is redemption.

Then we had to make it clear also that the nonviolent resister seeks to attack the evil system rather than individuals who happen to be caught up in the system. And this is why I say from time to time that the struggle in the South is not so much the tension between white people and Negro people. The struggle is rather between justice and injustice, between the forces of light and the forces of darkness. And if there is a victory it will not be a victory merely for fifty thousand Negroes. But it will be a victory for justice, a victory for good will, a victory for democracy.

Another basic thing we had to get over is that nonviolent resistance is also an internal matter. It not only avoids external violence or external physical violence but also internal violence of spirit. And so at the center of our movement stood the philosophy of love. The attitude that the only way to ultimately change humanity and make for the society that we all long for is to keep love at the center of our lives. Now people used to ask me from the beginning what do you mean by love and how is it that you can tell us to love those persons who seek to defeat us and those persons who stand against us; how can you love such persons? And I had to make it clear all along that love in its highest sense is not a sentimental sort of thing, not even an affectionate sort of thing.

Agape Love

The Greek language uses three words for love. It talks about *eros*. *Eros* is a sort of aesthetic love. It has come to us to be a sort of romantic love and it stands with all of its beauty. But when we speak of loving those who oppose us we're not talking about *eros*. The Greek language talks about *philia* and this is a sort of reciprocal love between personal friends. This is a vital, valuable love. But when we talk of loving those who oppose you and those who seek to defeat you we are not talking about *eros* or *philia*. The Greek language comes out with another word and it is *agape*. *Agape* is understanding, creative, redemptive good will for all men. Biblical theologians would say it is the love of God working in the minds of men. It is an overflowing love which seeks nothing in return. And when you come to love on this level you begin to love men not because they are likable, not because they do things that attract us, but because God loves them and here we love the person who does the evil deed while hating the deed that the person does. It is the type of love that stands at the center of the movement that we are trying to carry on in the Southland—*agape*.

Some Power in the Universe That Works for Justice

I am quite aware of the fact that there are persons who believe firmly in nonviolence who do not believe in a personal God, but I think every person who believes in nonviolent resistance believes somehow that the universe in some form is on the side of justice. That there is something unfolding in the universe whether one speaks of it as an unconscious process, or whether one speaks of it as some unmoved mover, or whether someone speaks of it as a personal God. There is something in the universe that unfolds for justice and so in Montgomery we felt somehow that as we struggled we had cosmic companionship. And this was one of the things that kept the people together, the belief that the universe is on the side of justice.

God grant that as men and women all over the world struggle against evil systems they will struggle with love in their hearts, with understanding good will. *Agape* says you must go on with wise restraint and calm reasonableness but you must keep moving. We have a great opportunity in America to build here a great nation, a nation where all men live together as brothers and respect the dignity and worth of all human personality. We must keep moving toward that goal. I know that some people are saying we must slow up. They are writing letters to the North and they are appealing to white people of good will and to the Negroes saying slow up, you're pushing too fast. They are saying we must adopt a policy of moderation. Now if moderation means moving on with wise restraint and calm reasonableness, then moderation is a great virtue that all men of good will must seek to achieve in this tense period of transition. But if moderation means slowing up in the move for justice and capitulating to the whims and caprices of the guardians of the deadening status quo, then moderation is a tragic vice which all men of good will must condemn. We must continue to move on. Our self-respect is at stake; the prestige of our nation is at stake. Civil rights is an eternal moral issue which may well determine the destiny of our civilization in the ideological struggle with communism. We must keep moving with wise restraint and love and with proper discipline and dignity.

The Need to Be "Maladjusted"

Modern psychology has a word that is probably used more than any other word. It is the word "maladjusted." Now we all should seek to live a well-adjusted life in order to avoid neurotic and schizophrenic personalities. But there are some things within our social order to which I am proud to be maladjusted and to which I call upon you to be maladjusted. I never intend to adjust myself to segregation and discrimination. I never intend to adjust myself to mob rule. I never intend to adjust myself to the tragic effects of the methods of physical violence and to tragic militarism. I call upon you to be maladjusted to such things. I call upon you to be as maladjusted as Amos who in the midst of the injustices of his day cried out in words that echo across the generation, "Let judgment run down like waters and righteousness like a mighty stream." As maladjusted as Abraham Lincoln who had the vision to see that this nation could not exist half slave and half free. As maladjusted as Jefferson, who in the midst of an age amazingly adjusted to slavery could cry out, "All men are created equal and are endowed by their Creator with certain inalienable rights and that among these are life, liberty and the pursuit of happiness." As maladjusted as Jesus of Nazareth who dreamed a dream of the fatherhood of God and the brotherhood of man. God grant that we will be so maladjusted that we will be able to go out and change our world and our civilization. And then we will be able to move from the bleak and desolate midnight of man's inhumanity to man to the bright and glittering daybreak of freedom and justice.

For Reflection

1. What kind of spirituality must be the foundation of any work for peace? Draw on both readings in your answer.
2. What assumptions and goals are shared by both the just-war theory and nonviolence? What are the key differences between the two traditions?
3. What elements of peacemaking do you draw on in your personal relationships with others? Which approach to peacemaking do your actions tend to reflect more—just war or nonviolence? Offer an example from your life to support your answer.

Profile

Christian Peacemaker Teams: Getting in the Way

Advocates of nonviolence suggest that it is most successful when it is practiced with as much training, planning, discipline, and sacrifice as any military would invest in its war making. One group that is willing to make such a commitment is Christian Peacemaker Teams (CPT), an ecumenical group that began in 1984 with the goal of enlisting Christians who would be willing to risk personal harm in order to intervene in violent situations. CPT's motto, "Getting in the way," refers to its commitment to following "the Way" of Jesus Christ. It also refers to what CPT members do—literally putting their bodies in harm's way in order to diffuse a violent situation, sometimes through direct intervention (standing in front of guns and tanks), but often simply by being peaceful witnesses who can influence events by reporting injustice to the rest of the world.

Working closely with local peace and human rights workers, Christian Peacemaker Teams travel to conflicts around the world. Eileen Hanson explains why she traveled with CPT to Palestine:

> At a checkpoint in Hebron, I stood talking with a young Israeli soldier who asked me "Why did you come to this 'God-forsaken' place?" . . . He guessed, correctly, that I could have chosen to visit lots of other places, to "live a comfortable life," as he said. I

could only respond by saying that I don't feel good about living such a life when I know others are denied it. . . . My faith calls me to be not only informed and concerned, but engaged in the world. (*Winona Catholic Reporter,* March 2006)

**Alexi Shephard,
a member of the Jesuit Volunteer Corps**

12

Social Doctrine and Ecclesial Action

Introduction

Now that you've sampled a good cross-section of the Catholic social justice tradition, it's time for a pop quiz. Working for justice in the world is the responsibility of:

a. people who have the power to change things—politicians, religious leaders, business executives, and the like
b. really holy people—Mother Teresa, Martin Luther King Jr., and so on
c. people who have the time and freedom to volunteer at food shelves and homeless shelters
d. all of us, each and every one

The answer, of course, is *d*—all of us, power brokers and ordinary citizens, saints and searchers, those with time to kill and those who barely find time to sleep. Responsibility for justice—the work of shaping society in a way that makes it easier for people to be good—belongs to everyone because everyone is a part of society. Everyone plays a role in shaping society through his or her daily choices. Even the choice to do nothing is a choice to keep things the way they are.

As the United States Catholic bishops point out in their 1998 pastoral letter *Everyday Christianity: To Hunger and Thirst for Justice: A Pastoral Reflection on Lay Discipleship for Justice in a New Millennium,* Christians have a special responsibility to work for justice because their Baptism unites them with Christ and calls them to carry on his mission in the world. It can be tempting to leave this mission to others—people more holy or powerful or free than we are. But it is actually in our ordinary, daily circumstances that we have the greatest effect on society.

It is in those ordinary circumstances that Christ calls on us to work for justice.

"Working for justice in everyday life is not easy," the bishops acknowledge in *Everyday Christianity*. The challenges of creating a better society were all too evident to Anna Nussbaum, a high school student from Colorado, as she reflected on a friend's abortion. But as she wrote in her award-winning essay "Axioms of Faith" (excerpted in this chapter) for *Commonweal* magazine, that is why faith makes all the difference. Because of her Catholic faith, Nussbaum realized that she is not called to change the world alone, but as part of a much larger community: the Church. More important, she says, faith transforms our vision. It opens our eyes to beauty, in every person and in the world at large. It opens our eyes to see new possibilities for the future, and it gives us the strength to choose those possibilities instead of just settling for the way things are. And ultimately, it gives us hope that we will someday see a world that is just as good as God intends it to be.

Excerpts from *Everyday Christianity: To Hunger and Thirst for Justice: A Pastoral Reflection on Lay Discipleship for Justice in a New Millennium*

by the United States Conference of Catholic Bishops

Introduction

One of the great challenges for Christians is as old as our faith, but it takes on special urgency today as we approach the third Christian millennium. How do we connect worship on Sunday to work on Monday? How is the Gospel proclaimed not only in the pulpits of our parishes, but also in the everyday lives of Catholic people? How does the Church gathered on the Sabbath act as the People of God scattered and active every day of the week? How can we best carry the values of our faith into family life, the marketplace and the public square? How do we love our neighbor, pursue peace, and seek justice in everyday choices and commitments?

> **third Christian millennium:**
>
> The third millennium (thousand-year period) after the birth of Christ, which began in the year 2001

In these reflections, we highlight one essential dimension of the lay vocation which is sometimes overlooked or neglected: the social mission of Christians in the world.[1] Every believer is called to serve "the least of these," to "hunger and thirst for justice," to be a "peacemaker."[2] Catholics are called by God to protect human life, to promote human dignity, to defend the poor and to seek the common good.

> **lay vocation:**
>
> The vocation, or calling, of the laity—all those who have been baptized but not ordained to the priesthood.

This social mission of the Church belongs to all of us. It is an essential part of what it is to be a believer.

This social mission is advanced in many ways—by the prophetic teaching of our Holy Father; by the efforts of our bishops' conference; and by many structures of charity and justice within our community of faith. But the most common—and, in many ways, the most important Christian—witness is often neither very visible nor highly structured. It is the sacrifice of parents trying to raise children with concern for others; the service and creativity of workers who do their best and reach out to those in need; the struggle of business owners trying to reconcile the bottom line and the needs of employees and customers; and the hard choices of public officials who seek to protect the weak and pursue the common good. The Church's social mission is advanced by teachers and scientists, by family farmers and bankers, by sales persons and entertainers.

The Catholic social mission is also carried forward by believers who join unions; neighborhood organizations; business groups; civic associations; the pro-life movement; groups working for justice; or environmental, civil rights or peace groups. It is advanced by Christians who stand up for the values of the Gospel. This mission is the task of countless Christians living their faith without much fanfare or recognition, who are quietly building a better society by their choices and actions, day by day. They protect human life, defend those who are poor, seek the common good, work for peace, and promote human dignity.

Working for justice in everyday life is not easy. There are complex and sometimes difficult challenges encountered by women and men as they try to live their faith in the world. We applaud the efforts of all Catholics to live the Gospel by pursuing justice and peace in their everyday choices and commitments.

The Catholic Layperson:
Discipleship and the Pursuit of Justice

Being a believer means that one lives a certain way—walking with the Lord, doing justice, loving kindness, living peaceably among all people. Christian discipleship means practicing what Jesus preached. Discipleship is found in a relationship with Christ and a commitment to His mission of "bringing glad tidings to the poor, / liberty to captives, / and recovery of sight to the blind / to let the oppressed go free."[3]

For Catholics, this takes on special meaning today. According to the Second Vatican Council, "It is the special vocation of the laity to seek the kingdom of God by engaging in temporal affairs and directing them according to God's will. They live in the world, in each and every one of the world's occupations and callings and in the ordinary circumstances of social and family life which, as it were, form the context of their existence. There they are called by God to contribute to the sanctification of the world within, like leaven, in the spirit of the Gospel, by fulfilling their own particular duties."[4]

temporal: relating to time; in this case, relating to things of the world, as opposed to things of the Church

We welcome and affirm the growing participation of lay women and men in the internal life of the Church. Service within the Church should form and strengthen believers for their mission in the world. With this pastoral statement we are addressing in a special way the demands of discipleship in the pursuit of justice and peace in everyday activity.

Followers of the Lord Jesus live their discipleship as spouses and parents, single adults and youth, employers and employees, consumers and investors, citizens and neighbors. We renew the warning of the Second Vatican Council, "One of the gravest errors of our time is the dichotomy between the faith which many profess and their day-to-day conduct."[5] By our baptism and confirmation every member of our community is called to live his or her faith in the world.

Called to Justice in Everyday Life

Catholicism does not call us to abandon the world, but to help shape it. This does not mean leaving worldly tasks and responsibilities, but transforming them. Catholics are everywhere in this society. We are corporate executives and migrant farm workers, politicians and welfare recipients, educators and day care workers, tradesmen and farmers, office and factory workers, union leaders and small business owners. Our entire community of faith must help Catholics to be instruments of

God's grace and creative power in business and politics, in factories and offices, in homes and schools, and in all the events of daily life. Social justice and the common good are built up or torn down day by day in the countless decisions and choices we make. This vocation to pursue justice is not simply an individual task; it is a call to work with others to humanize and shape the institutions that touch so many people. The lay vocation for justice cannot be carried forward alone but only as members of a community called to be the "leaven" of the Gospel.

- Our **families** are the starting point and the center of a vocation for justice. How we treat our parents, spouses, and children is a reflection of our commitment to Christ's love and justice. We demonstrate our commitment to the Gospel by how we spend our time and money, and whether our family life includes an ethic of charity, service, and action for justice. The lessons we teach our children through what we do as well as what we say determines whether they care for the "least among us" and are committed to work for justice.[6]

- **Workers** are called to pursue justice. In the Catholic tradition, work is not a burden, not just how we make a living. Work is a way of supporting our family, realizing our dignity, promoting the common good, and participating in God's creation. This means often doing the ordinary well, making the most of our talents and opportunities, treating others fairly and with dignity, and working with integrity and creativity. Believers should be encouraged to choose their work based on how they can best use the gifts God has given them. Decisions made at work can make important contributions to an ethic of justice. Catholics have the often difficult responsibility of choosing between competing values in the workplace. This is a measure of holiness. Associations that enable workers, owners or managers to pursue justice often make the witness of the individual more effective.[7]

- **Owners, managers, and investors** face important opportunities to seek justice and pursue peace. Ethical responsibility is not just avoiding evil, but doing right, especially for the weak and vulnerable. Decisions about the use of capital have moral implications: Are companies creating and preserving quality jobs at living wages? Are they building up community through the goods and services they provide? Do policies and decisions reflect respect for human life and dignity, promote peace, and preserve God's creation? While economic returns are important, they should not take precedence over the rights of workers or protection of the environment. Investors should examine ownership, management, and economic decisions in the light of the Catholic call to protect life, defend those who are poor, and seek the common good. These decisions promote human dignity or undermine it.[8]

- As **consumers,** believers can promote social justice or injustice. In an affluent culture that suggests that what we have defines who we are, we can live more simply. When we purchase goods and services, we can choose to support companies that defend human life, treat workers fairly, protect creation, and respect other basic moral values at home and abroad. We can also make conscious efforts to consume less.[9]

- All human beings have unique talents, gifts from God that we are called to develop and share. We should celebrate this diversity. People who use their skills and expertise for the common good, the service of others, and the protection of creation, are **good stewards** of the gifts they have been given. When we labor with honesty, serve those in need, work for justice and contribute to charity, we use our talents to show our love—and God's love—for our brothers and sisters.[10]

- As **citizens** in the world's leading democracy, Catholics in the United States have special responsibilities to protect human life and dignity and to stand with those who are poor and vulnerable. We are also called to welcome the stranger, to combat discrimination, to pursue peace, and to promote the common good. Catholic social teaching calls us to practice civic virtues and offers us principles to shape participation in public life. We cannot be indifferent to or cynical about the obligations of citizenship. Our political choices should not reflect simply our own interests, partisan preferences or ideological agendas, but should be shaped by the principles of our faith and our commitment to justice, especially to the weak and vulnerable. The voices and votes of lay Catholics are needed to shape a society with greater respect for human life, economic and environmental justice, cultural diversity, and global solidarity. Catholic involvement in public life and legislative advocacy are important ways to exercise responsible citizenship. Participation in politics is a worthy vocation and a public trust. Believers who serve in public office have unique responsibilities and opportunities to stand up for human life and dignity, to pursue justice and peace, and to advance the common good by the policies, priorities, and program they support or oppose.[11]

Conclusion

The Word of God calls believers to become "the salt of the earth, the light of the world."[12] The pope and the bishops are called to teach and lead, but unless the Church's social teaching finds a home in the hearts and lives of Catholic women and men, our community and culture will fall short of what the Gospel requires. Our society urgently needs the everyday witness of Christians who take the social demands of our faith seriously. The pursuit of justice is an essential part of the Catholic call to holiness, which is our true vocation: to live "in Christ" and let Christ live and work in our world today.

Christian faith requires conversion; it changes who we are, what we do, and how we think. The Gospel offers "good news" and guidance not just for our spiritual lives, but for all the commitments and duties that make up our lives. Living our faith in the ordinary tasks of everyday life is an essential part of what it means to be holy today.

As the third Christian millennium approaches, the call to live our faith in everyday choices and actions remains at the heart of what it means to be a disciple of Jesus. This call takes on renewed urgency as we approach the great jubilee, but it is not new. The task of disciples today was probably best and most simply expressed in the words of the prophet Micah:

"He has told you, O mortal, what is good;

and what does the LORD require of you

but to do justice and to love kindness,

and to walk humbly with your God?"

(Mi 6:8)

Endnotes

1. Other major documents address in a more comprehensive way the vocation of the laity (e.g., the *Dogmatic Constitution on the Church, the Decree on the Apostolate of the Laity, Called and Gifted, Called and Gifted for the Third Millennium*). Catholic teaching also outlines our broader social mission in a series of documents (e.g., *Pastoral Constitution on the Church in the Modern World, Justice in the World, On the Hundredth Anniversary of Rerum Novarum, A Century of Social Teaching, Communities of Salt and Light, Called to Global Solidarity*).

2. Matthew 25:31–46; Matthew 5:1–10.

3. Luke 4:18.

4. Vatican II, *Dogmatic Constitution on the Church (Lumen Gentium)*, no. 31.

5. Vatican II, *Pastoral Constitution on the Church in the Modern World (Gaudium et Spes)*, no. 43.

6. For more, see *On the Family (Familiaris Consortio)*, Pope John Paul II.

7. For more, see *On Human Work (Laborem Exercens)*, Pope John Paul II.

8. For more, see *Tenth Anniversary Edition of Economic Justice for All*, U.S. Catholic Bishops.

9. Ibid.

10. For more, see *To Be a Christian Steward*, U.S. Catholic Bishops.

11. For more, see *Octogesima Adveniens*, Pope Paul VI; *Political Responsibility*, U.S. Catholic Bishops.

12. Matthew 5:13–14.

Excerpts from "Axioms of Faith"

by Anna Nussbaum

In mathematics one must accept certain axioms, certain truths. Ten in all. Most important, one must accept the theoretical concepts of a point, a line, and a plane. Their existence cannot be proved or disproved, but they are the beginning of understanding geometry. My instructor explained, "You can't prove anything from nothing. . . . When you write a dictionary, if you don't have any words, you can't define any words."

We're a generation trying to write a dictionary of belief without words. Spoiled. Confused. Unwanted. Unformed. We have no place from which to begin. But faith persists, and all around me I find believers. . . .

I am at a party. A lot of people are drinking and, after a few beers, they have announced that they will not raise their children in a religious tradition. (I've noticed that when people are drunk they like to talk about God.) "I would just never do that to my kids," one says. "I'd let them decide for themselves about God. I wouldn't force it down their throats." They are passing on to their children the only religion they know, the religion of choice. This is a faith that makes them feel, as one of them says, "not really a part of any culture," that is, except a part of the consumer culture. They will raise their children to have choices. To survey the goods and choose the best buy.

For my peers, religion is but one choice in a world of choices. For me it is my beginning. It is the very soil in which I was planted. It is what happens every day. It is the prayers I say, or don't say. It is the questions I ask, the rituals I do. It is my parents. It is Sundays and holy days of obligation. It is the seasons. It is the source of frustration. It is dinnertable conversation. It is bad singing. It is my siblings. It is my identity. It is my limitation. It is the lens through which I was taught to see. It is my culture. I still choose every day, as my friends do. But I choose knowing that God expects something from me, and wondering what it is. I was raised Roman Catholic and that will never change, though it has changed me.

I have two dear friends, Avi Goldman and John Thomas Ritter. Avi is Jewish. After his mother died of cancer, Avi was very angry at God. Still, he celebrated his bar mitzvah. His father and sister don't practice. He goes to temple alone. For two years after Avi's mother died, his father took him and his sister around the world. They slept in a tent and got around on public transportation. Avi was eleven at the outset and turned twelve on the trip. He has ten journals from that time. Avi wasn't raised to be religious, but Indonesia, India, and Thailand turned him into a passionate boy, and a believer. He struggles with the particulars, but still seeks to live a life of faith because he witnessed so many believers in his journeys and saw, firsthand, the limitlessness of God's creation.

John Thomas used to live in Massachusetts, where he attended Bethany Brethren Chapel. He doesn't talk about his faith with me or anyone else at school. Mostly, he just lives it. His mother and sister dress modestly. His family doesn't own a television set or a secular music collection. He misses jokes about sitcoms and rap music. When I am a guest at his house, at dinner with his family, the boys pull out the chairs for all the ladies, even their little sister.

The three of us—John, Avi, and I—are an unlikely trio. A conservative Protestant, and a reform Jew, and a Catholic feminist—sounds like the beginning of a bad joke. I am considerably more rebellious than the two of them, neither of whom dates. It's true that outside of school we often hang with different crowds. But we are still the best of friends because we are involved in a never-ending conversation. We share a common vocabulary of faith. We laugh with each other. We speak freely. I have more in common with Avi and John Thomas, with Muslims and Mormons, than with those who feel that every religion can be purchased, or returned for a full refund. Or with those who believe that every religion can be discarded on the basis of logic. Or with those for whom diets, or achievements, take highest priority. . . .

It is an IB flex day and we don't have class. We are supposed to use this time to catch up on our studies. Avi turns to me in the library and asks me if I'll go for a hike with him. I am glad for an excuse not to do my homework. We drive to the mountains and start hiking the Mount Cutter Trail in Cheyenne Canyon. We make small talk, but I keep thinking about a friend's abortion. Avi asks me what I think about it. Avi is pro-choice. It's hard to have this conversation; most people just avoid talking about abortion. It's too painful. As soon as friends become sexually active, 'most everyone knows someone who has had an abortion.

I need to speak, but don't know what I think or what I should say. So that day I tell Avi I think we, as a community, can do better than abortion. I tell him that abortion degrades women, and kills children, and haunts my friends. It haunts me. I tell him it asks too much of young girls. I tell him society forces girls and women to feel that they should take part in this honor killing; that remaining childless protects their integrity, their choices in life. I tell him all this, feeling that my church hasn't done enough to stop it, or to prevent it, or to change it. I tell him all this knowing that I am a part of the problem, and that I have not been there to help. It feels good to speak about it even though I know how strongly Avi disagrees.

The air is thin and crisp. We hike faster until our breathing becomes labored. The conversation winds its way to the top of the hill and off the trail. It climbs over rocks, and runs down the gravel to the road. Finally, Avi understands where I am coming from. I say something like "every life is sacred." He says, "Yeah. You're right. But I don't think I could live it. . . . I mean the real world doesn't work that way. . . . If it was my girlfriend, I'd still want her to have the abortion." Avi believes abortion is right in a wrong sort of way. But even if it is wrong, he can't live it, this belief, all alone. The society tells him it's supposed to be that way: one person, one choice. It's supposed to be true that the continuation of a pregnancy is every single woman's choice, but it's not. Husbands, bosses, boyfriends, bills decide. And alone we choose out of desperation and, well, loneliness.

Being Catholic doesn't give me the answers, but it does give me the questions. It gives me courage to ask hard questions because I'm not alone. "What if your best friend got pregnant tomorrow?" Avi asks. "I don't know," I answer. "I guess she'd have the baby." Easier said than done, but not impossible. In the lonely, fend-for-yourself world, maybe it's impossible. But in a family, a community, a friendship, a tradition where "these things happen," where miracles happen, where you are worth more than your résumé, anything seems possible. Where wine is turned into blood. Where forgiveness happens. Where the rich housewife and the homeless man drink from a single cup. And a dead man was resurrected to ascend into heaven. Where people, however flawed and foolish, believe, everything seems a little more possible. If this community can believe that the dead will rise again can they also believe that the child of an unmarried teen mother can be loved, can be valued, can be good?

One Holy Thursday the church lady asked me if I'd come up from my pew and have my feet washed. They needed someone from my demographic. Why not? I thought it would be fun. I sat on the stoop between a deaf Hispanic man who looked homeless and an elderly Polish immigrant who struggled with his shoes and socks. I looked out at the congregation. I saw some kids from my high school. I saw all their stories. The one who had to come. The one who came alone. The one who came because he loves the pomp, the kitsch, the culture of it all. The one whose mother is so depressed that she didn't get out of bed that day or the day before that or the day before that. The one whose mother is dead. They were all singing this sweet, haunting melody, *"Ubi caritas et amor, Deus ibi est."* The Polish man sat like a child on the step with his pants legs rolled up. When his turn came, one priest held his hands gently under the man's little white and blue legs, the other poured clear water over his bony old feet and yellowing toenails. Then the bishop leaned down and kissed the man's feet as he had kissed mine. The man wept, moaned, and cried out.

> *Ubi caritas et amor, Deus ibi est:*
>
> in Latin, "Where charity and love are, God is there."

Moral axioms make mathematical axioms seem simple. No axiom is proved, so it requires imagination. I walk out into the night. Clean feet. Light heart. Maybe it was the singing or the quiet, or the men on the stoop, or the babies sleeping, but my eyes feel open. Open to see miracles. I look up and see the black sky, and the big white moon. I close my eyes and see the pews and the sea of people. I'm not alone, and under this sky seems a big enough place to begin.

For Reflection

1. In *Everyday Christianity,* under the heading "Called to Justice in Everyday Life," the United States bishops discuss how justice might be lived out in various roles that people have in everyday life. Choose one of those roles and describe how the principles of Catholic social teaching might transform the way someone carries out that role. Draw on the ideas in other chapters of this book to support your answer.
2. What role does faith play in how people see the world, and how they work for justice? What is unique about the way Catholics work for justice as a result of their faith? Draw on both readings to support your answer.
3. What are your own "axioms of faith"—those things you believe to be true, even if you cannot prove them? How does your faith influence your commitment to practice justice in the world?

Profile

Jesuit Volunteer Corps: Boot Camp for Everyday Christianity

Call it boot camp for living Christian justice in everyday life. The recent college graduates who volunteer with the Jesuit Volunteer Corps spend a year or more living very simply in small communities while serving in a wide variety of settings. Jesuit Volunteers join with various organizations and agencies to work with children, victims of domestic abuse, prisoners, homeless people, refugees, mentally disabled people, those struggling with HIV/AIDS, and whole communities. During their period of service, they draw on the spirituality of the Society of Jesus, the action-oriented religious order founded by a former military commander, Saint Ignatius Loyola, in 1540. In particular, the Jesuit Volunteer Corps emphasizes four ideals—community, simple living, spirituality, and social justice—that volunteers often carry into the rest of their lives.

- **Community.** Jesuit Volunteers live together in groups of four to eight people—and in the process, they consciously practice the skills necessary to form a community. "A J.V.C. community is not a group of individuals who are doing service and happen to be living together," explains David E. Nantais, S.J., who has worked with the Jesuit Volunteer Corps in Detroit. "Rather, the community empowers each volunteer to perform that service, and their experiences bring them together to reflect, pray and support one another" (*America: The National Catholic Weekly* Web site).

- **Simple living.** Jesuit Volunteers practice the preferential option for the poor (see chapter 7) by living in poor, underserved neighborhoods. Moreover, they receive only a small monthly stipend, and are encouraged to live as simply as possible. "A simple lifestyle is recommended not as an exercise in fortitude, to see who can get by on the least resources (like an inner-city version of "Survivor"), but rather to impel the volunteers to raise questions," says Nantais. "How much does one human being really need? Upon whom do I rely for my needs? What more should I do for others?" (*America: The National Catholic Weekly* Web site).

- **Spirituality.** Spirituality is an integral part of the Jesuit Volunteer experience. Volunteers are offered time for prayer and retreats, and the tools they need to reflect on their service experiences in the light of faith. In this way, they learn about the reciprocal relationship of prayer and action: just as prayer should inspire and sustain action for justice, "the hardships and graces of ministry are the substance for honest and holy dialogue with God in prayer," says Nantais (*America: The National Catholic Weekly* Web site).
- **Social justice.** Jesuit Volunteers get practical, hands-on experience working for justice in their volunteer settings. Although they come to serve, Nantais says it is not long before "they discover that glorious paradox of ministry: one receives far more than one gives" (*America: The National Catholic Weekly* Web site).

Some former Jesuit Volunteers came up with an informal, ironic motto for the Corps: "Ruined for life." They mean that in a good way: after a year of living the ideals of community, simple living, spirituality, and social justice, they find it difficult to live any other way.

Appendix

Additional Reading

The Church documents excerpted in this book represent only a small part of Catholic social teaching. A sample of additional Catholic social teaching documents is listed below, arranged by topic. Vatican documents are listed first, followed by documents of the U.S. Catholic bishops, in chronological order. As of this writing, all of the documents are available online, usually (but not always) at the Vatican Web site *(www.vatican.va)* or the United States Catholic bishops' Web site *(www.usccb.org)*.

Abortion
Declaration on Procured Abortion, Sacred Congregation for the Doctrine of the Faith, 1974
The Gospel of Life (Evangelium Vitae), John Paul II, 1995
Living the Gospel of Life, United States Conference of Catholic Bishops, 1998

Criminal Justice
Message for the Jubilee in Prisons, John Paul II, 2000
Responsibility, Rehabilitation, and Restoration: A Catholic Perspective on Crime and Criminal Justice, United States Conference of Catholic Bishops, 2000

Death Penalty
The Gospel of Life (Evangelium Vitae), nos. 27 and 56, John Paul II, 1995
Homily at the Trans World Dome, no. 5, John Paul II, 1999
Declaration of the Holy See to the First World Congress on the Death Penalty, Holy See, 2001
A Culture of Life and the Penalty of Death, United States Conference of Catholic Bishops, 2005

Development

On the Development of Peoples (Populorum Progressio), Pope Paul VI, 1967

On Social Concern (Sollicitudo rei socialis), Pope John Paul II, 1987

World Hunger, a Challenge for All: Development in Solidarity, Pontifical Council Cor Unum, 1996

A Place at the Table: A Catholic Recommitment to Overcome Poverty and to Respect the Dignity of All God's Children, United States Conference of Catholic Bishops, 2002

Economic Life

On Christianity and Social Progress (Mater et Magistra), Pope John XXIII, 1961

On the Hundredth Anniversary of Rerum Novarum (Centesimus annus), Pope John Paul II, 1991

A Decade After Economic Justice for All, United States Conference of Catholic Bishops, 1995

Socially Responsible Investment Guidelines, United States Conference of Catholic Bishops, 2003

End-of-Life Issues

Declaration on Euthanasia, Sacred Congregation for the Doctrine of the Faith, 1980

The Gospel of Life (Evangelium Vitae), nos. 27 and 56, Pope John Paul II, 1995

Address to the Participants in the International Congress on Life-Sustaining Treatments and Vegetative State, Pope John Paul II, 2004

Nutrition and Hydration: Moral and Pastoral Reflections, United States Conference of Catholic Bishops' Committee for Pro-Life Activities, 1992

Environment

Message for the Celebration of the World Day of Peace: Peace with God the Creator, Peace with All of Creation, Pope John Paul II, 1990

Common Declaration on Environmental Ethics, Pope John Paul II and Ecumenical Patriarch Bartholomew I, 2002

Global Climate Change: A Plea for Dialogue, Prudence, and the Common Good, United States Conference of Catholic Bishops, 2001

Family

Pastoral Constitution on the Church in the Modern World (Gaudium et Spes), nos. 47–52; Second Vatican Council, 1965

Letter to Families, Pope John Paul II, 1994

Putting Children and Families First: A Challenge for Our Church, Nation, and World, United States Conference of Catholic Bishops, 1991

Follow the Way of Love, United States Conference of Catholic Bishops, 1993

Gender Equality

Pastoral Constitution on the Church in the Modern World (Gaudium et Spes), nos. 29 and 49; Second Vatican Council, 1965

Apostolic Letter on the Dignity and Vocation of Women (Mulieris Dignitatem), Pope John Paul II, 1988

Letter to Women, Pope John Paul II, 1995

Strengthening the Bonds of Peace: A Pastoral Reflection on Women in the Church and in Society, United States Conference of Catholic Bishops, 1995

Health

Contemplate the Face of Christ in the Sick, Pope John Paul II, 2000

Health and Health Care, United States Conference of Catholic Bishops, 1981

A Framework for Comprehensive Health Care Reform: Protecting Life, Promoting Human Dignity, Pursuing the Common Good, United States Conference of Catholic Bishops, 1993

Human Rights

Peace in the World (Pacem in Terris), Pope John XXIII, 1963

Declaration on Religious Freedom *(Dignitatis Humanae)*, Second Vatican Council, 1965

Statement on the Fiftieth Anniversary of the Adoption of the Universal Declaration of Human Rights, Archbishop Theodore E. McCarrick, 1998

See also the United Nations' Universal Declaration of Human Rights, which has been strongly supported by Church leaders.

International Relations

Pastoral Constitution on the Church in the Modern World (Gaudium et Spes), nos. 83–90, Second Vatican Council, 1965

Address to the Fiftieth General Assembly of the United Nations Organization, Pope John Paul II, 1995

Ethical Guidelines for International Trade, Holy See, 2002

Called to Global Solidarity, United States Conference of Catholic Bishops, 1997

A Call to Solidarity with Africa, United States Conference of Catholic Bishops, 2001

Liberation

Medellín Documents, Conference of Latin American Bishops, 1968

Instruction on Certain Aspects of the Theology of Liberation, Congregation for the Doctrine of the Faith, 1984

Instruction on Christian Freedom and Liberation, Congregation for the Doctrine of the Faith, 1986

Migrants and Refugees

Refugees: A Challenge to Solidarity, Pontifical Council for the Pastoral Care of Migrants and Itinerant People and the Pontifical Council Cor Unum, 1993

The Church and Undocumented Migrants and Refugees, Including Those Who Are Not Christians, Pontifical Council for the Pastoral Care of Migrants and Itinerant People, 2002

Welcoming the Stranger Among Us: Unity in Diversity, United States Conference of Catholic Bishops, 2000

Strangers No Longer: Together on the Journey of Hope, Catholic Bishops of Mexico and the United States, 2003

See also the annual papal messages for the World Day of Migrants and Refugees.

Peace

Peace on Earth (Pacem in Terris), Pope John XXIII, 1963

Pastoral Constitution on the Church in the Modern World (Gaudium et Spes), nos. 28, 77–90, Second Vatican Council, 1965

The Challenge of Peace: God's Promise and Our Response, United States Conference Catholic Bishops, 1983

Message for the World Day of Peace 2004 ("An Ever Timely Commitment: Teaching Peace"), Pope John Paul II, 2004

See also the other papal messages issued for the World Day of Peace (January 1) annually since 1968; these may be found on the Vatican Web site by searching for "World Day of Peace."

Political Life

Pastoral Constitution on the Church in the Modern World (Gaudium et Spes), nos. 73–76, Second Vatican Council, 1965

Address on the Jubilee of Government Leaders, Members of Parliament and Politicians, Pope John Paul II, 2000

The Participation of Catholics in Political Life, Congregation for the Doctrine of the Faith, 2002

Catholics in Political Life, United States Conference of Catholic Bishops, 2004

Racial Equality

Pastoral Constitution on the Church in the Modern World (Gaudium et Spes), nos. 29 and 49, Second Vatican Council, 1965

The Church and Racism: Contribution to World Conference Against Racism, Racial Discrimination, Xenophobia, and Related Intolerance, Pontifical Council for Justice and Peace, 2001

Brothers and Sisters to Us, United States Conference of Catholic Bishops, 1979 (At the time of this writing, the United States Conference of Catholic Bishops was expected to issue a new pastoral letter on racism.)

Reproductive Issues

On Human Life (Humanae Vitae), Pope Paul VI, 1968

Instruction on Respect for Human Life in Its Origin and on the Dignity of Procreation, Sacred Congregation for the Doctrine of the Faith, 1987

Declaration on the Production and the Scientific and Therapeutic Use of Human Embryonic Stem Cells, Pontifical Academy for Life, 2000

Document of the Holy See on Human Cloning, Holy See, 2004

Work

Pastoral Constitution on the Church in the Modern World (Gaudium et Spes), nos. 63–72, Second Vatican Council, 1965

On Human Work (Laborem Exercens), Pope John Paul II, 1981

On the Hundredth Anniversary of Rerum Novarum (Centesimus annus), Pope John Paul II, 1991

See also Labor Day statements of the United States Conference of Catholic Bishops (issued annually and available at the Web site of the United States Conference of Catholic Bishops).

Violence

Message for the World Day of Peace 2002 ("No Peace Without Justice, No Justice Without Forgiveness"), Pope John Paul II, 2002

When I Call for Help: A Pastoral Response to Domestic Violence Against Women, United States Conference of Catholic Bishops, 1992

Confronting a Culture of Violence, United States Conference of Catholic Bishops, 1994

Walk in the Light: A Pastoral Response to Child Sexual Abuse, United States Conference of Catholic Bishops, 1995

Vocation of the Laity

Decree on the Apostolate of the Laity (Apostolicam Actuositatem), Second Vatican Council, 1965

On the Vocation and the Mission of the Lay Faithful in the Church and in the World (Christifideles Laici), Pope John Paul II, 1988

Communities of Salt and Light: Reflections on the Social Mission of the Parish, United States Conference of Catholic Bishops, 1993

Called and Gifted for the Third Millennium, United States Conference of Catholic Bishops, 1995

Acknowledgments

The scriptural quotations contained herein are from the New Revised Standard Version of the Bible, Catholic Edition. Copyright © 1993 and 1989 by the Division of Christian Education of the National Council of the Churches of Christ in the United States of America. All rights reserved.

The quotation on page 11 and the essay by Marion Maendel on pages 18–24 are from "Dorothy Day's Pilgrimage Continues at Casa Juan Diego: The Pilgrimage Continues . . . Poor Teach Harsh and Dreadful Love: A Disillusioned Catholic Worker Stays On," from the *Houston Catholic Worker* newspaper, at *www.cjd.org/paper/poor.html*, accessed October 31, 2006. Used with permission of Marion Fernandez-Cueto.

The quotations on pages 12 and 44 and the Excerpts from *Pastoral Constitution on the Church in the Modern World (Gaudium et Spes),"* numbers 1; 10; and 12–14, 19, and 22, in *Vatican Council II: The Basic Edition, Constitutions, Decrees, Declaration,* revised edition, edited by Rev. Austin Flannery, OP (Northport, NY: Costello Publishing Company), pages 163, 171–172, 174–175, 175–177, 180, 185–187, 189–190, and 180, respectively. Copyright © 1996 by Costello Publishing Company, Inc., Northport, NY. Used with permission of the publisher. All rights reserved. No part of these excerpts may be reproduced, stored in a retrieval system, or transmitted in any form or by any means—electronic, mechanical, photocopying, recording, or otherwise—without express permission of Costello Publishing Company, Inc.

The quotation on page 28 and the section titled "Excerpts from *Justice in the World*" on pages 29–32 are from *Justice in the World,* by the World Synod of Catholic Bishops, numbers 6, and 1–6 and 29–38, at *www.osjspm.org/justice_in_the_world.aspx*, accessed October 22, 2006.

The section titled "Excerpts from *Voice of the Voiceless: The Four Pastoral Letters and Other Statements"* on pages 33–38 are from *Voice of the Voiceless: The Four Pastoral Letters and Other Statements,* by Archbishop Oscar Romero, translated from the Spanish by Michael Walsh (Maryknoll, NY: Orbis Books, 1993), pages 73–75 and 79–80. Copyright © 1985 by Orbis Books. Used with permission.

The quotation by Jean Donovan on pages 39–40 is from *Blessed Among All Women: Women Saints, Prophets, and Witnesses for Our Time,* by Robert Ellsberg (New York: Crossroad Publishing Company, 2005), page 312. Copyright © 2005 by Robert Ellsberg.

The excerpt by Pope John Paul II on page 44 is from Homily at the Trans World Dome, number 5, at *www.vatican.va/holy_father/john_paul_ii/travels/documents/hf_jp-ii_hom_27011999_stlouis_en.html*, accessed October 22, 2006.

The section titled "'With a Human Being Who's About to Be Killed'" on pages 52–57 is from the article "With a Human Being Who's About to Be Killed," by Sr. Helen Prejean, in *Peacework,* April 2000, volume 27, number 304, pages 6–8. Used with permission.

The section titled "Excerpts from the Message for the 1999 World Day of Peace" on pages 45–51and the quotation on page 58 are from the Message for the 1999 World Day of Peace," numbers 1–13 and 12, by Pope John Paul II, at *www.vatican.va/holy_father/john_paul_ii/messages/peace/documents/hf_jp-ii_mes_14121998_xxxii-world-day-for-peace_en.html*, accessed October 22, 2006.

The excerpt on pages 58–59 is from *Witness: Writings of Bartolomé de Las Casas,* edited and translated by George Sanderlin (New York: Orbis Books, 1992), page 67. Copyright © 1971 by George Sanderlin.

The quotations on page 62 and the section titled "Excerpts from 'Building Solidarity: From Rwanda to the Asian Tsunami'" on pages 69–74 are from "Building Solidarity: From Rwanda to the Asian Tsunami," on the Catholic Relief Services Web site, at *www.crs.org/about_us/newsroom/speeches_and_testimony/releases.cfm?ID=22,* accessed October 22, 2006.

The section titled "Excerpts from *Sharing Catholic Social Teaching: Challenges and Directions*" on pages 63–68 is from *Sharing Catholic Social Teaching: Challenges and Directions,* by the United States Conference of Catholic Bishops (USCCB), on the USCCB Web site, at *www.nccbuscc.org/sdwp/projects/socialteaching/socialteaching.htm,* accessed October 22, 2006. Used with permission.

The quotation on page 63 is from the English translation of the *Catechism of the Catholic Church* for use in the United States of America, number 1397. Copyright © 1994 by the United States Catholic Conference, Inc.—Libreria Editrice Vaticana. Used with permission.

The quotations by Eileen Egan on page 75 are from "Eileen Eagan, Pacifist, Helped Start Pax Christi," by Antonia S. Malone, in the *National Catholic Reporter,* October 20, 2000, volume 37, issue 1, page 7.

The quotations on pages 77 and 93 are from "Couples Help Couples: Movement Grows Again," by Robert McClory, in the *National Catholic Reporter,* September 4, 1998, volume 34, issue 38, pages 20–22.

The bulleted items on page 78 and the section titled "Excerpt from *The Role of the Christian Family in the Modern World (Familiaris Consortio)*" on pages 79–84 are adapted and taken from *The Role of the Christian Family in the Modern World (Familiaris Consortio),* by Pope John Paul II, numbers 18–27, 28–41, 42–48, and 49–64, respectively, at *www.vatican.va/holy_father/john_paul_ii/apost_exhortations/documents/hf_jp-ii_exh_19811122_familiaris-consortio_en.html,* accessed October 22, 2006.

The section titled "Excerpt from *A Christian Theology of Marriage and Family*" on pages 85–92 is from *A Christian Theology of Marriage and Family,* by Julie Hanlon Rubio (New York: Paulist Press, 2003), pages 186–193. Copyright © 2003 by Julie Hanlon Rubio. Used with permission of Paulist Press, *www.paulistpress.com.*

The bulleted items on human work on page 96 are adapted from *On Human Work (Laborem Exercens),* numbers 4, 9, 27, and 10 at *www.vatican.va/edocs/ENG0217/_INDEX.HTM,* accessed October 22, 2006.

The section titled "Excerpts from *Economic Justice for All: Pastoral Letter on Catholic Social Teaching and the U.S. Economy*" on pages 97–104, the section of the same name on pages 117–121, and the quotation on page 116 are from *Economic Justice for All: Pastoral Letter on Catholic Social Teaching and the U.S. Economy,* numbers 96–106 and 110–116; 85–95; and 13; respectively, by the USCCB, at *www.osjspm.org/economic_justice_for_all.asp.,* October 22, 2006. Copyright © by the USCCB, Inc. Used with permission.

Excerpts from "'By Their Fruits You Shall Know Them: Can Catholics Make a Difference for Justice in the Business World?'" on pages 105–111 is from "By Their Fruits You Shall Know Them: Can Catholics Make a Difference for Justice in the Business World?" by Dennis O'Connor, in *U. S. Catholic,* May 2004, pages 12–13 and 14–17. Used with permission.

The section titled "Excerpt from *We Believe in the God of Life: Gustavo Gutiérrez*" on pages 122–124 is from *The God of Life: Gustavo Gutiérrez,* translated by Matthew O'Connell (New York: Orbis Books, 1991), pages xi–xiii. Copyright © 1991 by Orbis Books. Used with permission.

The section titled "Excerpt from *A Theology of Liberation: History, Politics, and Salvation*" on pages 125–130 is from *A Theology of Liberation: History, Politics, and Salvation,* revised edition, by Gustavo Gutiérrez, translated by Sr. Caridad Inda and John Eagleson (New York: Orbis Books, 1988), pages 171–173. Copyright © 1973, 1988 by Orbis Books. Used with permission.

The excerpt on page 131 is by Mike Sersch. Used with permission.

The quotations by President Clinton on page 133 are from "Bernardin Awarded Medal of Freedom," in *National Catholic Reporter*, September 20, 1996, volume 32, issue 40, page 4.

The quotation by Cardinal Joseph Bernardin on page 134 and the section titled "Excerpt from 'The Public Life and Witness of the Church'" on pages 143–149 are from "The Public Life and Witness of the Church," in *America*, October 5, 1996, volume 175, issue 9, pages 15–25. Copyright © America Press, Inc. Used with permission. For subscription information, visit *www.americamagazine.org*.

The section titled "Excerpts from *Faithful Citizenship: A Catholic Call to Political Responsibility*" on pages 135–142 is from *Faithful Citizenship: A Catholic Call to Political Responsibility*, by the USCCB, on the USCCB Web site, at *www.usccb.org/faithfulcitizenship/bishopStatement. html*, accessed October 22, 2006. Copyright © USCCB, Inc. Used with permission.

The quotation on page 154 and the section titled "Excerpts from *Peace on Earth (Pacem in Terris)*" on pages 155–161 are from *Peace on Earth (Pacem in Terris)*, numbers 112 and 80–89, 91–93, 98–100, and 120–125, by Pope John Paul XXIII, on the Vatican Web site, at *www.vatican.va/holy_father/john_xxiii/encyclicals/documents/hf_j-xxiii_enc_11041963_ pacem_en.html*, accessed October 22, 2006.

The section titled "'Nobel Lecture'" on pages 162–165 is from "Nobel Lecture," by Kim Dae-jung, in Oslo, Norway, December 10, 2000, at *nobelprize.org/peace/laureates/2000/ dae-jung-lecture.html*, accessed October 22, 2006. Copyright © 2000 by the Nobel Foundation. Used with permission.

The quotation by Lindy Boggs on page 167 is adapted from an interview with the *Pittsburgh Post-Gazette*, April 23, 2001, page D2.

The second quotation by Lindy Boggs on page 167 is from "Public Service a Higher Calling," in the *Times Union* newspaper, November 7, 1999, page A6.

The quotation about the Grand Canyon on page 169 is from the Environmental Movement History Web site, at *www.ecotopia.org/ehof/timeline.html*, accessed October 22, 2006.

The information about the bald eagle on page 169 is from the CNN.com Web site, at *www. cnn.com/NATURE/9907/02/bald.eagle.02/*, accessed October 22, 2006.

The information about the chemical plant on page 169 is from the Guardian Unlimited Web site, at *www.guardian.co.uk/international/story/0,1755603,00.html*, accessed October 22, 2006.

The quotation by Pope Paul VI on page 169 is from *Octogesima Adveniens*, number 21, at *www.vatican.va/holy_father/paul_vi/apost_letters/documents/hf_p-vi_apl_19710514_ octogesima-adveniens_en.html*, accessed October 22, 2006.

The section titled "Excerpts from *Renewing the Earth: An Invitation to Reflection and Action on Environment in Light of Catholic Social Teaching*" on pages 171–178 is from *Renewing the Earth: An Invitation to Reflection and Action on Environment in Light of Catholic Social Teaching*, by the USCCB, on the USCCB Web site, at *www.usccb.org/sdwp/ejp/ bishopsstatement.htm*, accessed October 22, 2006. Copyright © USCCB, Inc. Used with permission.

The section titled "'Environmental Justice: A Catholic Voice'" on pages 179–183 is taken from "Environmental Justice: A Catholic Voice," in *America*, January 19–January 26, 2004, volume 190, issue 2, page 12. Copyright © America Press, Inc. Used with permission. For subscription information, visit *www.americamagazine.org*.

The excerpt on page 184 is from *Small Is Beautiful: Economics as if People Mattered*, by Ernst Friedrich Schumacher (Point Roberts, WA: Harley and Marks Publishers, 1999), page 249. Copyright © 1973 by E. F. Schumacher.

The section titled *"The Harvest of Justice Is Sown in Peace: A Reflection of the National Conference of Catholic Bishops on the Tenth Anniversary of the Challenge of Peace"* on pages 189–199 is from *The Harvest of Justice Is Sown in Peace: A Reflection of the National Conference of Catholic Bishops on the Tenth Anniversary of the Challenge of Peace*, by the

Photo Credits